From the same author:

The Silence of an Eloquent Soul (Poetry, 2002)

The Peppers (Shorts Stories, 2004)

Le Tambour des Tabous (Short Stories, 2008)

To my father, **Seldieu Loriston**, originally from Ile-de-la-Tortue (Tortuga), and my loving mother, **Yvanette Joseph**, originally from Saint Louis du Nord, for the passion with which they protected and nurtured my childhood and allowed me to grow up with honesty as my compass.

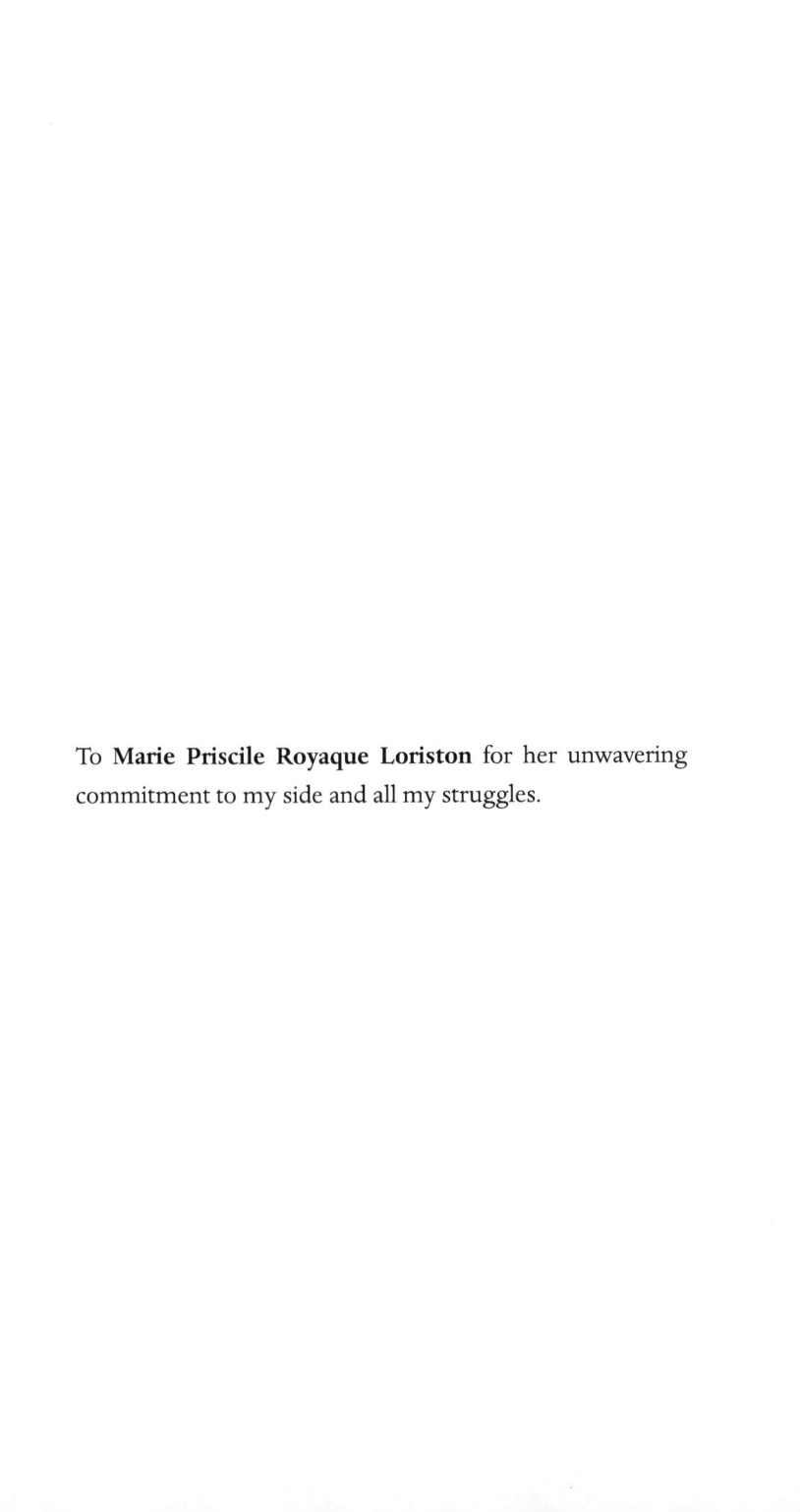

To **Marie Priscile Royaque Loriston** for her unwavering commitment to my side and all my struggles.

To my daughter **Dallyah Audrey LORISTON (DAL),** who, from the first wave of emotions I felt at her birth, activated a new dimension of my humanity and continues to allow me to experience the power of paternal love.

Thank you to all the teachers who held my hand in primary school at the Lamennais school in Saint-Louis du Nord and secondary school at the Lycée Tertullien Guilbaud in Port-de-Paix.

I am grateful for my professors at the various university centers I have attended: they have helped me develop a particular taste for science and the span and underpinnings of knowledge and have allowed me to sharpen my intellectual acumen.

Special thanks to Professor Esau John the Baptist for his uncommon esteem and trust!

To Cassandre Sophia AMAN, Esau JEAN BAPTISTE, Robens MAXI, specially Kevin H. JOSEPH from TransIn Services, for revising the English version of this book.

To **Sulfrida M. DUMESLE** for his devotion, critical reading of this text, and unconditional support!

TABLE OF CONTENTS

Acknowledgements.. 12
Author's words.. 14
Preface.. 20

CHAPTER I
HUMAN COMPETENCE

Human Competence.. 29
Knowledge, Intelligence, and Competence............................... 31
Technical Competence... 32
Human Competence.. 33
The Notion of clean Intelligence and Pure Knowledge............ 34
What happens to man?... 36
An observation.. 37
Can man recover his human competence? 40

CHAPTER II
HONESTY

Honesty can be learned and cultivated..................................... 47
Spare the rod and spoil the child.. 48
The Contribution of Religious Education
to Moral Formation.. 49
The Punitive Approach in Moral Formation............................ 52
The Contribution of Philosophy in Moral Formation.............. 53
Get inspired by good deeds.. 55
My First Steps Towards Financial Independence
and the Temptation to be Dishonest... 59

Go from 0 to 12,000 gourdes... 60
Confronted with dishonesty... 61
Dishonest people are willing to do anything............................. 63
Go from $300 to $1000... 64
Go from $1000 to $1500... 65
Latest full-time work experience.. 66
The path to honesty is a hard fight... 67
The Power of Haitian Witchcraft in Destruction...................... 69
How did we know what was going on?...................................... 71
Oh my God! Men are wicked... 71
A second "strike.".. 72
God can use all man-made tools to work miracles................... 73
Be honest at all times.. 74
Testing as a source of learning.. 80
A simple reading made me understand everything.................. 81
Something clicked in December 2020.. 82
Everything exists from its opposite.. 85
Being honest also means paying a full tithe.............................. 86
Boiler Pâté: Equilibrium price... 88
We can achieve our most ambitious dreams by following
the path of honesty... 91
Holding the bar for honesty.. 92
Promoting a culture of honesty.. 93

CHAPTER III
NEUTRALITY IN THE FACE OF INJUSTICE
DOES NOT EXIST

Let Us Love the Truth... 101
The Truth Is Expensive... 104
Let Us Love Justice.. 105

Defending justice even in favor of one's enemies.................... 107
Silence when facing injustice is a greater injustice................. 109
The slightest resistance weakens injustice............................. 111
Complicit through silence... 112

CHAPTER IV
THE MIRACLE OF HONESTY

A Way of Seeing Things.. 121
It's never too late... 123
The Miracle of Honesty.. 124
Honesty, love, and empathy go hand in hand......................... 127
Honesty as a source of mutual aid... 128
Honesty as the victory of the soul over the body................... 130
Annex I.. 133
Annex II... 137

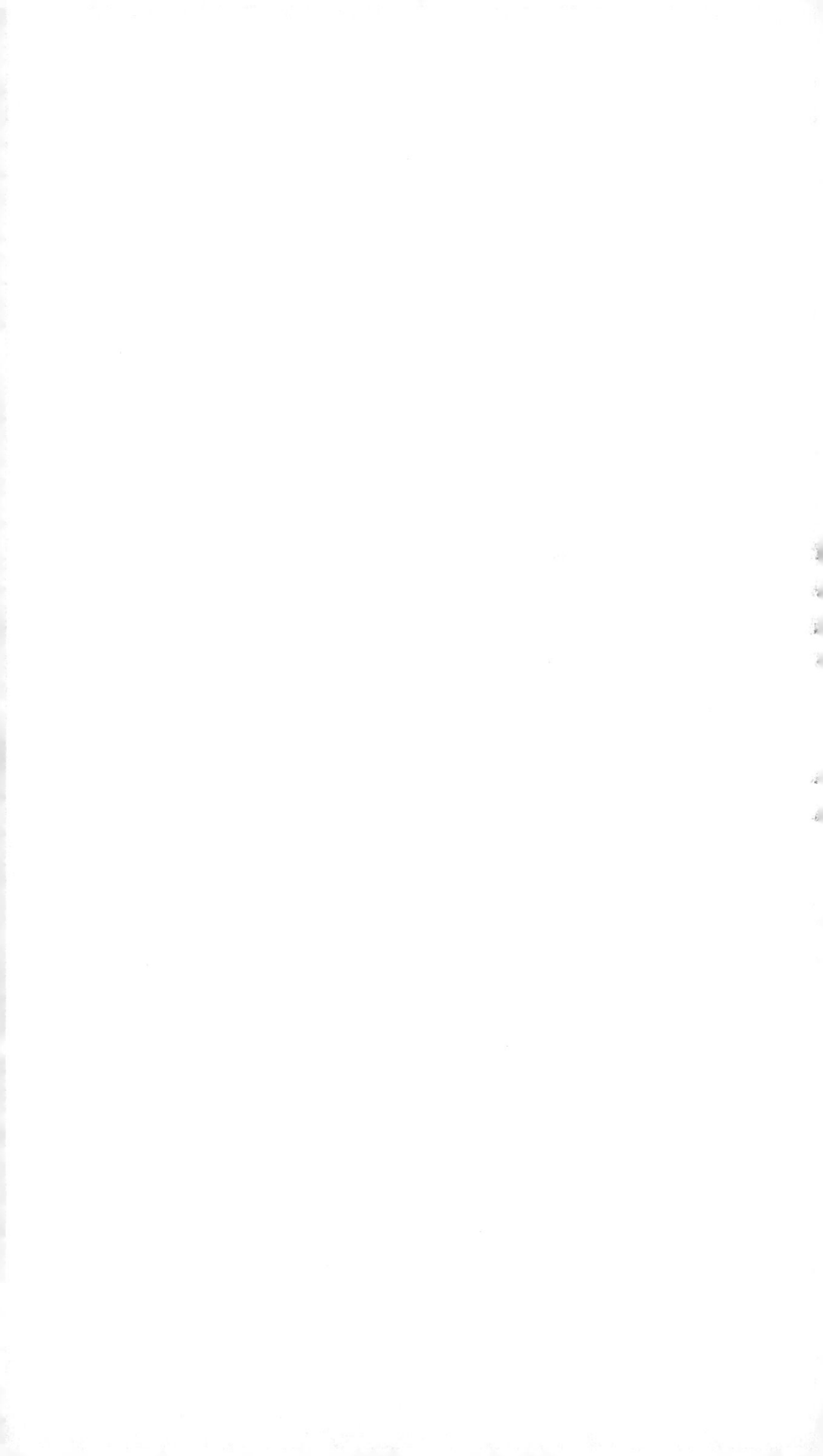

Acknowledgements

I dedicate the entire content of this book to all those who really know me and witness the immense efforts I make every day to remain candid, even in situations where it has not been evident. For their support and trust, I would like to thank: **Wilgens DEVILAS, Emma Loriston, Marc André LORISTON, Wilenda SAINDIC, Yrvin LORISTON, Evenel MOROSE, Dackmar EUGENE, Mildride FAUSTIN, Rolnor CHALITE, Michedalie CALIXTE, Izzy, Gueldy LAURENT, Micheline FRANCOIS, Wilmide GEORGES, Solange MAUVAIS, Ermann SAINVIL, Bendy GENESTANT, Djuno CADET, Linda Pierre AMEUS, Sandina Gabrielle JEAN-MARY, Stepher Roseberdie DEREME, Elizabeth**

The miracle of honesty

Etienne BASTIEN, Kattia SAINT-HILAIRE, Louis-Dalès DESSENTIEL, Marc-Enson JOSEPH, Miclaude PAUL, Benito FERMINE et **Migne-Yourdide M. JASMIN** aka **Maizu**.

I would also like to express my gratitude to **Valéry Numa, Michenet BALTAZAR, Jocelyn TITUS, Seide JEAN-CLAUDE, Fanilien GUILLAUME, Richard SIMEUS, Jude SIMEUS, Pierre Agenor CADET, Jackson JOSEPH, Fresnel JEAN, Rock CLAVAROCHE, Ricardin ST-JEAN, Jean Claude THERVIL, Fresnel ALCIME, Chelet NORELIEN, Boubet LOUIS-PIERRE,** Althery Etienne, **Marc F. SHAPIRO, Amiel DUFRESNE, Enork RAPHAEL, Dieunou MAURICE, Elianne BENOIT, Marie-Ange PIERRE, Holdine PIERRE, Ferlandanie CORNEILLE, Rodrigue RAYMOND, Gorétie METAYER, Frantz R. ROMOND, Nickel JEAN, Dérilien MERIZIER, Evelt SAINVIL, Kwesi KORREH, Evolution Law Group, HD MRI, Bob LORISTON, Julien JULMISTE, Yveny et Fausia LORISTON, Wedzer VERTULMA, Gerdine FRANCIQUE, Fadnet JEAN-BAPTISTE, Mark L. SHAPIRO,** Tonald Capita, **Hongueur ELUSMA, Samuel PIERRE LOUIS, Guerby CIMIL, Dorothy VERLISSAINT, Guy Webern GUERRIER,** Leslie Gélin, **Yeldie ALCINDOR, Riquet ALCINDOR, Agabus JOSEPH, François Carleb LORISTON, Richardson HONORÉ, Beaugé LAURENT,** Thériel Thelus, Marie Raphaëlle Pierre, Alangue Valbrun, **Yolande TURENNE, Nadyne JEAN, Gabart E. SAINTIL** all the collaborators of my different companies, my supporters of the diaspora, all my readers!

Author's words

As I am writing the first page of this book, which is intended to make a plea for the need for a culture of honesty, I am 40 years old. I'm going to tell you about your life by telling you about mine. Each of my readers will be able to find a part that corresponds closely to a slice of his life. The events I am recounting may take place in a different space or area than yours, but I am sure that you will recognize yourself in them and may even think that someone close to you has told me your own story. That is not the case!

Nor is this book a coming-of-age novel. I have gone to great lengths to resist the pull of fiction. I will only tell you about my experiences, the lessons I have learned, the failures I have experienced, my humble origins, my religious upbringing, my inclinations toward philosophy, and my exploits.

The miracle of honesty

In this literary adventure, you will notice my passion for values like **loyalty, justice, empathy, honesty, truth, love, greatness of soul, self-esteem, mutual aid, intelligence, and moral strength.**

I don't just deal with these topics in this book, but I put a lot of effort into making them lanterns that guide me in every moment of my life. I am a sinner like every man on earth. But I know that we are all endowed with the power to overcome our desires and weaknesses. We are capable of being pleasant in a world characterized by ugliness where morality is becoming old-fashioned.

My dearest wish is that this book will become a source of hope and motivation for my readers. Thus, they will be endowed with the power to encourage honest people to go it alone without ever allowing themselves to be swayed by the so-called modern and widespread wave of justified misconduct. Today the world isn't a healthy place. The advent of social networks, far from democratizing knowledge, is bringing about regrettable changes that are leading the world's youth down a dangerous slope that compromises the future of humanity and future generations. All this is taking place under the powerful eyes of the new masters of the world, to repeat the famous sociologist, Jean Ziegler.

With bitterness in my soul and sometimes tears that fall on each key of my computer, I write this book to raise awareness among all who will read it. You should know that my tears abounded when, in some pages of this book, I spoke of the injustices, the betrayals of which I have been a victim despite my kind heart, despite the unconditional love that I have always offered to those around me and to every person I have met throughout my life.

I didn't cry because the harm done to me hurts. No! My tears came as I reflected on the profanities of the modern world, the dehumanization and human incompetence that afflict our contemporaries. I've always wondered. How can anyone do that? How does it feel like? What's the thought process? What's the motive?

It was believed that modern time inventions and the birth of new information and communication technologies would only improve and fluidify interaction between the members of humanity and consequently improve their living conditions. Yet, they seem to carry an unprecedented global social disorganization. Far from facilitating social harmony between social groups, social networks only dissect social relations and deconstruct with rare ease the values on which human society is based. No one foresaw that the mobile phone (cellular) connected to the Internet would transform each individual either into a journalist, a scholar capable of intervening on all subjects, even those related to science, or into a professional liar who can say anything, without any coercion, to murder the character of another person he does not even know. Often, these changes have a detrimental impact on life in society, and the previously and conventionally established rules constitute powerful obstacles to virtues such as truth, justice, loyalty, empathy, and love. All these virtues are replaced by confusion, delusion, celebrity syndrome, love of easy money, and pretense.

The findings are frightening, certainly, but should we lose all hope? Should we leave the future of humanity in the sole hands of the unlearned, the automatons who invade social networks? No!

Scientists, sociologists, governments, philosophers, computer scientists, programmers, and socio-professionals must plan an invasion of social networks and a transcendental reform of these essential and fragile tools. In the same way, a gun will never be left in the hands of a child, no matter how intelligent they may be. The use of the powerful weapons of new information and communication technologies cannot just be handed over to anyone who wants it. The use of these tools of mass transformation must be limiting and rigorously conditioned. I insist a little on digital inventions not to show that they are not – all-important – but to draw everyone's attention to the contribution of these tools to the spread of bad morals at an incredible speed from one society to another. From one age group to another.

This book, intended to resonate with honesty, will generally deal with the notions of human skills, good, evil, and injustice. In this work, I address the subjects that fascinate me and on which I am firmly convinced. I am telling you a small amount of my experience in the earthly adventure and the struggles I am waging in a challenging country like Haiti.

In the second chapter, I will tell you a little about myself and my career without excess or invention. Moreover, in this book, unlike my previous works, I am saddened by not being able to make room for poetry, imagination, or fiction. I'm limited to telling verifiable facts and experiences. In some parts, I will mention the names of some still alive and well-known personalities. I will only recount facts as examples supporting my visceral attachment to the first of all human skills: Honesty. I will also recount the experiences of some people who marked my youth: their actions symbolize this virtue that is becoming rarer day by day.

Finally, I thank you for agreeing to read the few words that make up this modest work, and I want to guarantee that you will find in it, ideas that make sense and the meaning of a battle that must involve all of us, in other words, the greatest number or a critical mass.

Long live honesty, long live justice, long live love and truth!
Daniel LORISTON

Preface

Our quest for evolution and progress often points to intelligence, as the means to get there. A quick observation will lead us to think of something else that is also needed and vitally important, known as consciousness.

Intelligence, while conferring the capacity of great achievement, can be easily put to the service of evil. It can rationalize injustice, justify exploitation, and devise ways of harming and taking advantage of others. Conscience, on the other hand, that inner light which guides our actions towards what is right and good, is the true antidote to mediocrity and destruction.

The miracle of honesty

As you are reading this book, I invite you to a profound exploration of consciousness, for therein lies the key to our true elevation as individuals and as a society. Recognize yourself in the author, Daniel Loriston. What he describes to us resembles the words of a fictional soldier who experienced war: "I have seen boys... their arms torn out; their legs ripped off. But there isn't anything like the sight of an amputated spirit; there is no prosthetic for that." (film Scent of a Woman, 1992). We are destroying the souls of our young Haitian men and women. What we're looking for is a form of human competence far more precious than what could be simply defined as "intelligence". It's pure knowledge, devoid of moral impurities, illuminated by the light of conscience and guided by irreproachable ethics. This is the true essence of our own intelligence.

The Miracle of Honesty is the long-awaited remedy that answers the insidious evil that is destroying our Haitian society and the world in which we live. We are not aware of the suffering that is within us, because it is relegated to the backyard. We are a nation plagued by a multitude of afflictions, but of all the remedies considered, this book contains the elixir. By embracing honesty as our guide, we commit ourselves to a path of transparency and integrity that promotes personal development and collective well-being. It's a conscious choice that strengthens the bonds between individuals and nurtures an environment that fosters growth and fulfillment.

When our institutions, companies, and governments act with integrity, they inspire public confidence and beget a climate of cooperation and harmony. Corruption, lies and deceit, on the other hand, undermine the foundations of social trust and jeopardize stability and progress.

Through the illuminating examples in this book, we are called to awaken, recognize, and understand the exact position of the evil that afflicts us. When The Miracle of Honesty is read in school and work environment, it will act like a sunrise, gradually dispelling the darkness and bringing dawn to our dear Haiti.

Kerving H. Joseph

THE MIRACLE OF HONESTY

DANIEL LORISTON

The miracle of honesty
Cover and layout : Brainkrea
ISBN : 9798884118584

All rights reserved

"Beeing honest may not get you a lot of friends, but it will always bring you the right ones."
Jhon Lennon

CHAPITRE I
Human Competence

In my daily life, and in the face of the problems faced by my country (Haiti), I often find myself obliged to answer questions from young people on the notion of competence. I myself have often questioned the competence of Haiti's contemporary ruling class.

In my various interventions as an opinion director and as a media boss, I have always had to mention that the last time the history of Haiti was confronted with intelligence and any kind of knowledge dates back to people with little education and barely literate: Jean Jacques Dessalines, Toussaint Louverture, General Capois La Mort and so on!

I can never understand how people who could barely read, could fight to allow the young Haitian nation to escape the slavery that was dumbing it down and to gain its Independence, when it seems impossible today to our scholars (for the most part, holders of master's and doctorates from the great universities of the world and of Haiti) to preserve this heritage by safeguarding our sovereignty.

Despite the expansion of the humanities in Haiti (sociology, law, political science, economics, anthropology, social work, etc.), the Haitian intelligentsia has not been able to solve a single problem in 30 years among all those that eat away at the existence of the Haitian people.

After more than two centuries and 20 years of the establishment of the post-colonial state, we are not even able to meet the most basic need of the Haitian people, namely "EAT." There is reason to doubt the knowledge conveyed in Haitian schools and universities.

We must doubt not only the knowledge supposedly imparted but also how it is to affect man by making him better. It can be noted that the Haitian education system, far from training men, only creates the monsters we know people who, by their actions, can only worsen or amplify the Haitian calamity.

To all those young people who often appreciate my interventions at conferences or radio broadcasts and who often ask me how "competent" personalities (university professors, intellectuals, lawyers, bureaucratic professionals, and technicians) can offer such mediocre results. The answer is always the same: despite their level of education, they lack judgment and pure knowledge!

The miracle of honesty

I believe the very short time I often have to answer such a complex question has always prevented me from providing edifying and unambiguous explanations. I will provide all the details about my understanding of the phenomenon in this reflection work, which is intended to be an exercise of grasping concepts, such as Knowledge, Intelligence, and Competence.

KNOWLEDGE, INTELLIGENCE, AND COMPETENCE

According to "Petit Larousse", **Knowledge** can be understood as a coherent set of information acquired in contact with reality. That is to say, to have the ability to practice after study and learning and to carry out an activity. Among all the definitions provided by the 'Petit Larousse' of the concept of **intelligence**, I retain this one: The ability of a human being to adapt to a situation to choose means of action according to the circumstances. Finally, **competency** is a recognized ability in a particular subject (field) because of the knowledge possessed, which gives the right to judge it.

A careful analysis of these typical dictionary definitions will lead to the conclusion that Competence is a combination of **both Knowledge and Intelligence.** Therefore, competent people have knowledge put into action with the help of Intelligence. Knowing everything requires a few skills.

We do not doubt that among the many Haitian leaders, some possess knowledge. For example, don't those who are lawyers and who work as ministers of justice or members of the cabinet of the minister of justice or as judges or public

Human competence | Chapitre I

defenders have a recognized ability in the field of law? If these brilliant lawyers we cherish are competent, why aren't they able to make the justice system better?

These questions can be raised for all other areas of public life. Our economists who have become governors of the Bank of the Republic of Haiti, our agronomists who have become ministers of agriculture, and so on, are they not often graduates of the major universities abroad and the State University of Haiti, which certify their studies with a bachelor's, master's or doctorate based on a global assessment of their competence?

And why, despite the certified skills of these well-known personalities, all we hear from them is that they swell the ranks of the corrupt and fuel corruption without the slightest concern for the results? To be technically proficient without being endowed with *intelligence of one's own and pure knowledge* is a monstrosity, pure and simple! Before stating my vision of the notion of clean or clear Intelligence and pure knowledge, it seems appropriate to try to establish the difference between two (2) distinct forms of competence: **Technical Competence and Human Competence**: the first refers to **know-how**, and the second to **deontology** (Ethics) or virtue.

TECHNICAL COMPETENCE

It expresses a **know-how** implemented to achieve a result or performance. The cabinetmaker has a technical skill that allows him to build a chair. The chair is a **result**, a performance. The Jurist, on the other hand, is a legal professional with technical competence that allows him to participate in the organization of society or simply the judicial system. The quality of the judicial system of court decisions is a result.

By extension of meaning, technical competence is the ability to do something in a specific area. The form in which this activity is carried out makes all the difference. The value of a professional or academic performance depends not only on its technical competence but also on its ethics. A professional is only recognized under technical competence and ethically appropriate behavior.

HUMAN COMPETENCE

Human Competence itself refers to ethics, which is intended to be the matrix of good professional behavior or a code of professional practice. It can be defined as the set of rules or values to be followed in the implementation of a technical skill.

The doctor, dressed in his white coat, who examines the sick (patient), exercises his technical competence. He holds a doctorate, which allows him to know the causes of the most well-known diseases in his community and follow the treatment protocol corresponding to each disease. But suppose this doctor refrains from telling the truth to his patient to prolong the treatment and get as much money as possible. In that case, he turns out to be a humanly incompetent health professional.

Human competence | Chapitre I

Human skills are the virtues attached to the personality of a morally responsible person practicing particular virtues. It is also the personal, human, and relational qualities that a person shows in the workplace. These qualities or virtues do not relate to diplomas or technical knowledge of a subject but rather to interpersonal skills. Human skills include Loyalty, honesty, empathy, benevolence, sensitivity, a sense of humanity, etc.

THE NOTION OF CLEAN INTELLIGENCE AND PURE KNOWLEDGE

By clean Intelligence and Pure Knowledge, **we mean** the combination of technical and human competence. A technically competent person who is not humanly competent is exhibiting discounted competence. Their technical competence then becomes a burden, a vice, a nightmare.

Humanity is populated by highly skilled and unquestionably technically proficient people, but unfortunately, this is not enough to make the world a better place than the one we have today. Moreover, the world as it is today the result of all the decisions and actions undertaken by these people (the lords of the world, to quote Jean Ziegler).

Clean intelligence or Pure Knowledge is the exercise of a technical competence supported by human competence, i.e., interpersonal, or ethical values. During my academic and professional career, I had the opportunity to cross paths with many great Haitian professors. I have never been so in

The miracle of honesty

touch with knowledge as when I attended the courses these distinguished professors gave.

In my heart, I was subtly trying to deify these exceptionally technically competent professors who captivated me with the art with which they taught their lessons. Once in the public administration, these professors act like ineffectual morons. On the contrary, instead of seeing any noticeable results or improvements in the public activity they are assigned to, we only hear about their involvement in corruption scandals. I have always had an incurable wound in my heart when their names were mingled in vast corruption cases.

I've always thought to myself how such a competent person could let his fame be tarnished. I have the answer today. Without human competence, technical competence is merely theoretical and akin to excessive cretinism.

Only technical competence mixed with human competence is capable of getting Haiti out of the dilemma it is in. We call this mixture of technical and human competence clean intelligence and pure knowledge, that is, knowledge incompatible with moral impurity and vices. In other words, knowledge or skill that sacrifices self-centeredness on the altar of the public interest. Let us transform Haiti through the experience of this new form of intelligence and knowledge.

Total Intelligence must be clean; Knowledge must be pure!

Human competence | Chapitre I

WHAT HAPPENS TO MAN?

Man in his finitude, that is, his limited existence, is prey to many temptations that risk making him lose the essence of his life, his mission, and at the same time, make him forget his skills related to the many challenges that await him on the path of mortal experience.

Originally, we are sent into mortality to make the earth better, share love, practice good and righteousness, and advance humanity from the perfectible man (bearing the seeds of perfection) that we are to the perfect man we aspire to be.

If we have agreed that we did not come to this earth by chance and that we almost certainly have a mission to accomplish, this automatically implies that we are endowed with power and the means to carry it out. And why is humanity deteriorating daily instead of improving through our actions? Why all the rumors of war in the world? Why is there so much famine in a world with a production surplus? Why is there this discrepancy between our **strengths**, our powers, and the quality of the human condition? The world as it stands today gives the image of a jungle where the big eat the small and where it is permissible to derogate from all the rules of law as long as one is powerful politically, economically, and militarily.

The military arsenal of regional power, far from serving to protect other small surrounding countries, serves as a constant threat on their backs and serves to destroy their already precarious economy and human lives of all ages and circumstances. Over the past three decades, we have seen the exercise of buccaneer, pirate, or mercenary diplomacy consisting of declaring war or bombing countries without a second-strike force or retaliation just to plunder their resources. The Western world, in its unhinged madness, thinks it has the right to massively take the lives of thousands of peaceful citizens who disagree with their political leaders. What folly! The images on television of the disastrous consequences of these invasions or military strikes give us an idea of the world's mental health.

AN OBSERVATION

The observation is that our pride, our desires, our desire to dominate, to kill, to have everything for ourselves, and our wildest fantasies put our human skills (those linked to our person) at half-mast. Our follies of all kinds make us castaways on this earth, whereas originally, we were only envoys with a clear mission: changing and transforming the world by making it better than before.

The human competence discussed in this chapter is a level of progression in relation to human values. Socrates, the Greek philosopher of the fifth century B.C., seems to explain best what I would like to imply here when he says that excellence is a virtue. The one (the philosopher) is considered virtuous if he acts with excellence, in other words, if he allows himself to be guided by reason. According to him (Socrates), excellence, understood here as a virtue, is the ability to live daily life according to a certain number of principles and values, the practice of which makes it possible to lead an acceptable moral life, in other words, a good life.

It is not given to all men to love their neighbors, to have respect for others, to have compassion for their fellow men, and to act loyally toward them. These human skills are acquired through education, effort, and willpower. This requires human competence to be able to exercise them. You must be humanly competent to know fraudulently taking someone else's thing is not an option. Having attained a high level of human competence (loyalty), even one who manages money and could steal a small sum without being suspected, doesn't allow himself to be carried away by temptation. Just because he's not a thief doesn't mean he won't do it, nor does fear deter him. He manages to remain in control of himself despite his financial problems because he is humanly competent. Thus, he has a strong moral conscience that prevents him from hating others for their progress, achievements, intelligence, talents, and achievements.

All the evils, the social scourges that eat away at humanity and disturb the world's peace, result from human incompetence. Let us imagine for a moment a world in which all leaders, decision-makers, and citizens, in general, are humanly competent and manage to act with loyalty to avoid any unreason by putting man at the center of all their actions.

The eminent intellectual and honorable senator of the 48th Haitian legislature, Eddy Bastien, writes in his book entitled

The miracle of honesty

"Reinventing the Republic" published in 2010, that the State must help promote and realize a culture of *"living together"* as one of the best ways to achieve social harmony and peace. I believe that with these remarks, the former senator wanted to insinuate that state actors must facilitate the cultivation of diversity of values, laws, and customs, the pooling of our strengths and capacities to exploit our shared resources for the benefit of the daughters and sons of the nation while guaranteeing equal opportunities and the equitable distribution of wealth.

It is essential to look at how the members of humanity tear each other apart and how the strong and more economically powerful Western countries strive to dominate, control, and plunder the wealth of less developed countries to establish instability and almost permanent chaos. When we observe, at a smaller level, the inability of the citizens of the same country to agree against their oppressors and predators, there is no doubt that the whole of humanity suffers from terrifying HUMAN INCOMPETENCE!

Man has become so incompetent that he cannot even retain what makes him a man: his humanity. By letting his humanity escape far from him, man unabashedly admits his human incompetence and his inability to preserve himself. I like this quote from the Dalai Lama, Tenzin Gyatso, spiritual leader of the Tibetans: *"We are interested in its members as parts of its body, why not in men as parts of humanity?"*

Human competence | Chapitre I

CAN MAN RECOVER HIS HUMAN COMPETENCE?

This decline in the floundering of the human species can be explained on several levels. However, in the context of our reflection, we want to point out the disconnection between man and nature and the rejection of ancestral values engendered by civilization and technological progress. It's not that man shouldn't evolve and sharpen his intelligence. Above all, we want to denounce the tendency of man to have recourse to modern science, technology, and industry to treat nature as an object. To repeat Max Weber, this mercantile savagery of contemporary technology and industry descending on nature has disenchanted the world.

Millennia before us, the people who inhabited the earth, revered nature, and adopted an attitude toward it that was both magical and religious. The trees that used to shade them are now in our bedrooms and living rooms in the form of tables, beds, and all kinds of furniture. The leaves of trees used by the first humans as natural medicines to efficiently drive away the ills that gnawed at the human body are now demonized, if not thrown to animals, in favor of the chemical poisons of the ultra-rich pharmaceutical world. The land is gutted, the rivers diverted, and the forests razed.

This total disorder initiated in the world based on modern technical and scientific progress would not remain without consequences. It promotes a loss of sensitivity towards animals, natural resources, the environment, and humans.

The miracle of honesty

The more the gap between nature and man widens, the more man loses his strength, deviates from his primary mission, puts the future of humanity in danger, and thus becomes incompetent in the face of his human responsibilities. I fully share the value of the Indian proverb: *"We did not inherit the land from our ancestors; we borrowed it from our children"*

Above all, I must not understand that I am minimizing the scientific and material progress that technology and technique are lagging. Rather, I argue that man must not continue to move at high speed towards a kind of prometheism in his desire to demonstrate power by opposing nature, by thinking that he can equal it. In doing so, man resembles a bird destroying the branch it lands or the niche that serves as its habitat.

My former literature teacher at the Lycée, the late Joseph Jacques Florvil, often liked to repeat a quote from Francis Bacon that I find very appropriate: *"One commands nature only by obeying it."* In the sense that man, being endowed with reason, must follow its rules, and conform to them to use it (nature) to his advantage.

This reconciliation with nature advocated by many thinkers can restore to humanity all its human skills and actual power over the future. Once man reconciles with nature, shows respect for it, and treats it not as an object but as a superior force, they will be freed from their primal animality. They will see their reason activated to the dimension of optimal human skills or values.

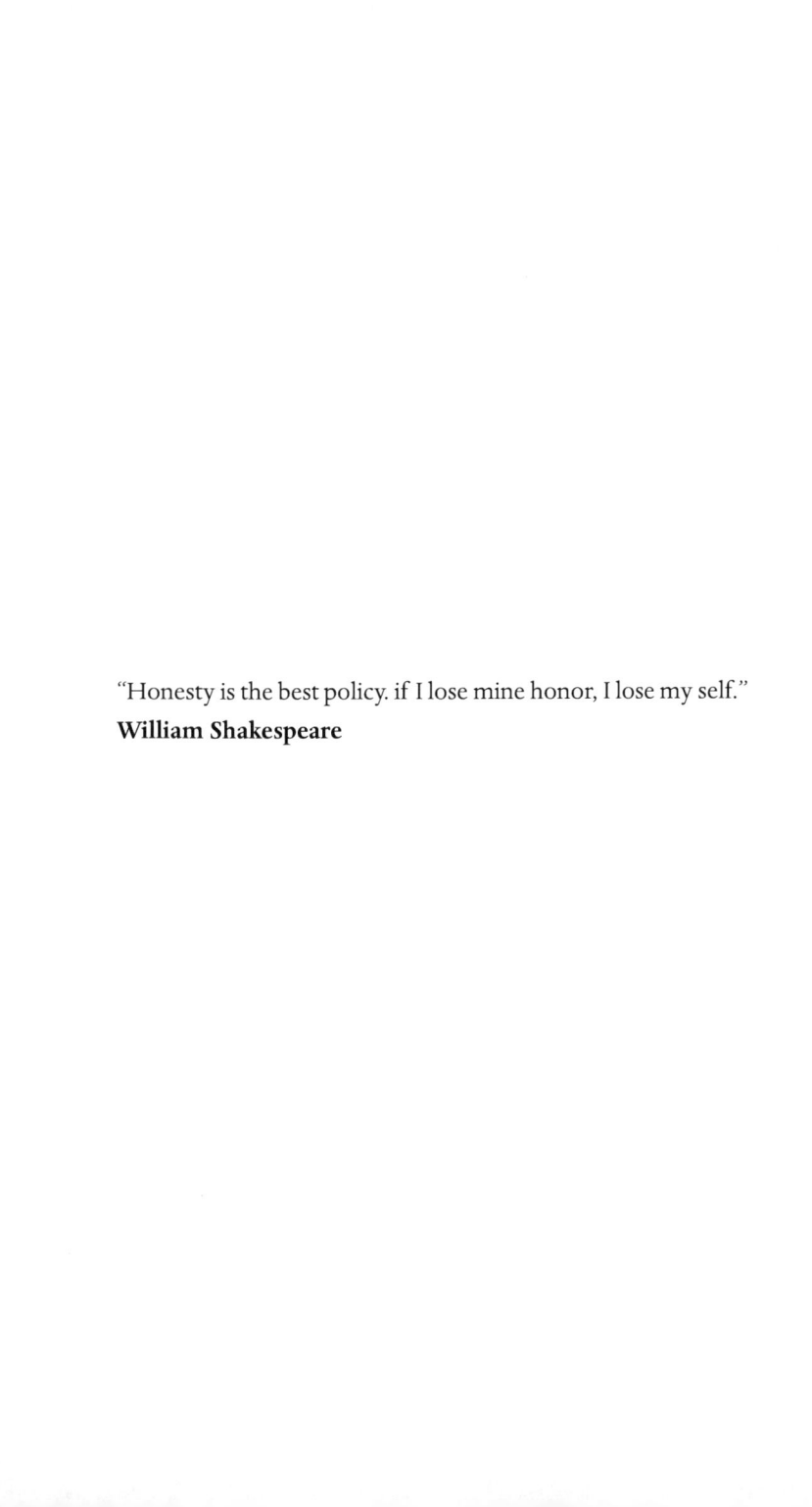

"Honesty is the best policy. if I lose mine honor, I lose my self."
William Shakespeare

CHAPITRE II
Honesty

"Honesty is a human skill."

"No one is capable of honesty as much as they are capable of detaching themselves from the world!"
Socrates

The miracle of honesty

HONESTY CAN BE LEARNED AND CULTIVATED

I was born into a modest family of Mormon Christian faith (Church of Jesus Christ of Latter-day Saints) to a father who had been a tailor since birth and a mother who was a small second-hand business. It was in the charming town of Saint Louis du Nord, at the bottom of the village, that I spent my childhood until the age of fourteen before being welcomed by the city of Port-de-Paix, where I did all my secondary education.

I had a controlled and supervised childhood. I couldn't play freely with the other neighborhood kids so that I wouldn't espouse their bad habits. According to my parents, any constant contact with children in whom Christian morality is not taught is a hindrance to other children.

Honesty | Chapitre II

To support and make this idea reasonable, my parents never tired of quoting Proverb 22, verse 6, *"Teach the child in the way he ought to go, and when he is old, he shall not turn away from it."*

I hear, as if it were today, the voice of my father, my hero, who always told us (we are four children) that a single rotten orange can spoil a whole basket full of good oranges! In my parents' eyes, we were not necessarily superior to other children, but rather, they were trying to establish a prevention mode through these teachings. In truth, not even the shadow of parental rigor that hung over us existed in the majority of the children of the neighborhood. They had a little more freedom than we had.

As kids, we couldn't do everything we wanted. We were obliged to act according to established rules and instructions. As soon as we exceeded the permissible limit, we were punished with the utmost severity.

SPARE THE ROD AND SPOIL THE CHILD

My loving mother and father, two human monuments, are the perfect model for parents who want nothing but suitable for their children. They were tough. Their corrections were severe. No kid in our neighborhood could experience more beatings than we did (tears fall from my eyes as I write this), but today, I understand that it was just another way to show their love for their children. So, this is what helps me understand the medieval Latin adage: **"Qui bene amat, bene castigat."** He who loves well chastises well!

The miracle of honesty

Since my father is an avid reader, especially the standard books (the Bible, the Book of Mormon, the Doctrine and Covenants, etc.), the Proverbs of Solomon did not work in our favor. My father remembered above all the following two passages: *"For the LORD chastises him whom he loves, as a father chastises the child whom he cherishes." (3:12)* or *"He who spares his rod hates his son, but he who loves him seeks to correct him." (13, 24)*. They hardened his punitive belief in education.

I was maybe 12 years old, and I wondered why the same action committed by another child in the neighborhood elicited laughter from his parents while the same action brought a "rain of whippings!" upon me. Today, at the age of 40, I see the difference between these children and me: I am a free adult, while many of these children who have become adults are in life in prison, are drugged, and die prematurely because of their excessive and disorderly behavior, etc.

My experiences teach me that honesty is learned and cultivated throughout life and that this virtue, in other words, this competence of the human soul, is not acquired automatically. Just as the baker uses a round pan to have a round loaf of bread, similarly if an individual has to use the mold of honesty to acquire human competence, this mold is first and foremost the family (the home).

THE CONTRIBUTION OF RELIGIOUS EDUCATION TO MORAL FORMATION

According to the requirements for Mormon parents, parents should organize religious education activities in the home to

Honesty | Chapitre II

instill moral and spiritual values in their children. Mormon doctrine teaches that parents will give an account of their children's doomsday if they do not show them the right path that leads to repentance, to a virtuous life, and above all, to eternal life. Let us be clear: parents are held responsible for children's misconduct if the effort to educate them has not been made.

In order not to be held accountable, my parents jealously obeyed these principles and organized routine activities that contributed to our education. Every morning, we had to go to our parents' room, kneel and pray to God. Thank Him for a good night spent, asking Him forgiveness for our deviations, protection during this new day, and the willingness to choose suitable over evil.

At this customary space, which we called morning devotion, my father would teach for at least 20 minutes a principle of the gospel, a moral value. He also shared the inspiration he received for his family. Sometimes, deeply affected by what he taught, he wept. Sometimes, the whole family would cry as if to thank the Holy Spirit for his visit and support. I can't count the times we (my two brothers, my little sister, and I) had to be late for school because the morning devotion lasted longer than usual.

Another activity that Mormons call "Family Home Evening" takes place every Monday night. All Mormon families are encouraged to host such activities once a week to teach the gospel in the home, discuss family decisions so that children can learn about them, provide feedback, and participate in decision-making. It's also a space where children have the chance to mention things they didn't like, and overly rigid decisions made by their parents over the past week. Parents, too, say the behaviors they didn't like and the changes they want to see.

After all these discussions, the whole family enjoys a small dinner prepared for this purpose. These family evenings are precious moments and constitute a space for consolidating the family and, above all, a channel for transmitting moral and spiritual values. I encourage all families worldwide to create spaces like this to teach children and pass on the correct values.

In these family gatherings, I learned the meaning and importance of honesty, loyalty, justice, truth, love, charity, compassion, and mutual aid. I also learned how to cultivate and internalize them. I grew up with these values as a clue to what is good. To this day, when faced with a situation where there are two options, I always ask myself which one is akin to loyalty. What is the choice of justice? Which side is the truth?

One can generally criticize the modern approach of some of today's churches that are plagued by human weaknesses, that is, human incompetence, and serve as mercantile enterprises for certain manipulative rulers. Yet the church, in many

Honesty | Chapitre II

respects, when led by men who have received the power of the Comforting Holy Spirit, serves to soften the human soul and is a mold in which the moral personality of the one who puts the teachings into practice is formed. The church provokes in the minds of the citizens an inevitable anguish of sin.

I testify that the teachings of The Church of Jesus Christ of Latter-day Saints (Mormon) have helped me grow in a certain rectitude and fear of losing all the eternal possibilities that lie before me if I refuse to live a righteous life where the effort of repentance is made daily. In the opinion of the Mormon Church, it is not that one should be without sin, but the important thing is to make amends for one's sins, forsake them, and repent of them. I confess with sincerity that these teachings have influenced my life and helped me cultivate as much as possible honesty, that human skill that we discuss in this chapter.

THE PUNITIVE APPROACH IN MORAL FORMATION

The home I grew up in wasn't a prison, but it wasn't a free space where children could afford to do whatever they wanted. Despite the spaces for discussion and teaching (morning devotional and weekly family home evening), my parents did not hesitate for a second when it came to correcting morals that were not in line with biblical precepts. This correction could be a good spanking, a severe verbal reprimand, deprivation of food for hours, standing on one foot for a quarter of an hour, or, at worst, depending on the seriousness of the offense, being locked up alone for hours in a room.

It was a form of isolation to tell the child that they were unsociable during this period and that because of the act done, they lost their rights and privileges for a certain time. These were moments of meditation and reflection for the child being punished this way. Locked in a room, he shed tears of regret.

I wonder how my parents transformed a room in which we liked to sleep into a prison cell. I must admit that these parental constraints imposed on us have made me an honest citizen. Honest in the slightest contact with others and with myself. Despite persecution, trouble, and hatred, I remain committed to this rare human skill.

THE CONTRIBUTION OF PHILOSOPHY IN MORAL FORMATION

Contrary to what a fringe of the Christian community would have us believe, philosophy does not systematically distance the one who practices it from God or the right path. In his book "A History of Philosophy," published in 2021, Luc Ferry, a French philosopher, explains how Schopenhauer sees philosophy not as a religion but a secular spirituality. That is to say, a spirituality without God! According to the Philosopher, religion pursues the same original objective as philosophy: *giving meaning to life and overcoming the metaphysical anguish linked to finitude (our lives are limited in time) by providing mortals with a definition of wisdom and the good life.*

Honesty | Chapitre II

The great themes of philosophy are justice, truth, honesty, the good and the beautiful, death, morality, etc. Are these not also the great themes of the Christian religion?

What differentiates philosophy from religion is that religion revolves around "FAITH," and philosophy around the clarity of "REASON." True, some philosophers do not believe in the existence of a God as a figure who overlooks everything as described by the Christian religion. Still, the divergence of views on the question of God in philosophy does not prevent philosophy from being the best partner of religion in its mission to make men good so they may be saved. In its quest for truth, philosophy aims only to make men better. And in its attempt to save man by exercising his reason, it becomes *"a doctrine of salvation without God."*

That part of general philosophy, which is called practical philosophy, is concerned only with the actions and activities of man. Just as moral philosophy, as a branch of practical philosophy, advocates the primacy of good over evil, all activities of the Christian religion are supposed to have the victory of good over evil as their ultimate goal. Hence, philosophy and the Christian religion meet! With this in mind, I wonder why this hatred of philosophy is being fed into the Christian milieu.

Besides the solid religious education I received, philosophy is the other field that has allowed me to strengthen my moral convictions and my strong sense of honesty. At the beginning of this chapter, I left you a thought of Socrates on honesty as an

The miracle of honesty

epigraph: *"No one is capable of honesty as much as he is capable of tearing himself away from the world, of being detached from it!"*

From Socrates' point of view, the individual must detach himself from the world to be capable of honesty. This implies that the individual must follow a set of rules and principles to avoid acting like ordinary mortals. He must distinguish himself from the world and proclaim its rarity by acting in the direction of goodness and truth; He vigorously rejects the ease into which the majority plunges.

Socrates uses the word capable advisedly to remind us that honesty is a skill, so only a minority will be able to do it. This minority will comprise all those learning this virtue and have made many efforts.

When, in my final year of high school at **Lycée Tertulien Guilbaud** in Port-de-Paix, where I was doing Philosophy A (literature section), I first became acquainted with philosophy thanks to professors **Enold JOSEPH and Eddy Bastien**, both from Saint Louis du Nord, I realized that this field was in some way complementary to my Christian moral formation. Perhaps I also fell deeply in love with it because philosophy did not distract me from what Christian education taught me about morality, honesty, justice, and loyalty. Philosophy is a way of life!

GET INSPIRED BY GOOD DEEDS

My former philosophy professor, Senator Eddy Bastien, is one of the few people with whom I had no family connection and

Honesty | Chapitre II

had the most significant influence on me regarding honesty and morality. This man's humility, remarkable simplicity, modesty, rejection of easy wealth, and habitual calmness bewitched me from our first contact. I actively participated in his electoral campaign 2006 as head of communication and the youth sector.

I wrote and produced election propaganda spots in this volunteer role, influenced young people to vote for him, and spoke at all public meetings. We ran an election campaign without the power of money. All that worked in our favor was that the honesty of the candidate, Eddy Bastien, was known to everyone, even to the peasants living in remote and difficult-to-access areas. I was strengthened when, in rural areas, young men and women stood up in the audience to say that Eddy Bastien was their teacher. They always took the opportunity to praise the honesty of this man. These testimonies made it easy and allowed us to win the hearts of voters with greater ease. He was elected to the North-West Senate.

A few months after his election, Senator Bastien was scheduled to travel to Saint Louis du Nord to participate in the patronal feast of his hometown, where many supporters had moved heaven and earth to help him obtain a massive vote. Usually, during the patron saint's festivals, the elected representatives are awaited by a huge crowd waiting to receive envelopes containing money. Senator Eddy Bastien faced a double problem: he was broke, so he couldn't make

The miracle of honesty

any generous gestures towards his supporters; moreover, not attending the traditional mass commemorating the patronal feast in the cathedral of Saint Louis King of France would be a wrong political move. On the advice of those close to him, including myself, he devised a strategy of not being seen in public before the official Mass.

I was in a small room at the senator's mother's house with his wife, Elizabeth Etienne, his older brother Jocelyn Bastien, and himself. There was no indication that the supporters would gather in front of the house's front door since the senator did not return triumphantly to the city, and the official vehicle was already hidden in a covered garage. Suddenly, a huge crowd arrived at the front door:
"Tell the senator that we are here." He already knows what we're looking for.
Pressures are mounting. The room becomes hot like a fiery furnace. We sweat profusely. These activists will never understand that a senator has no money to offer them, the senator's wife mutters. The minutes tick by. No one dares to come out and say a word to these already disgruntled activists.
An angel passes by to use a French expression describing a moment of total silence, and the senator's phone rings. A citizen of the department, known for his links to drug trafficking, calls him.
-Senator Eddy Bastien, how are you holding up?
"We're here; we're just coping," replies Eddy Bastien
"Senator, I know you are in the area; please lend me your

official vehicle for 45 minutes. When I return it, I'll give you an envelope of 40,000 US dollars!
"I can't lend it to you; it's an official vehicle granted by the Haitian government," retorts Eddy Bastien!

It takes a strong morale and a strong sense of loyalty and honesty not to succumb to these powerful temptations. This event changed my youth and increased my admiration for Eddy Bastien. I still recall other actions that testify to the former senator's deep commitment to his unwavering moral convictions. I am not alone in praising the former parliamentarian's loyalty. He is one of the few Haitian elected officials from 2006 until today who does not carry the weight of any suspicion of corruption, embezzlement, excess of power, or illicit enrichment on his back.

Indeed, his humility and disinterestedness in easy wealth were a source of ridicule during his tenure. Yet, today, we cannot afford to talk about honest politicians in Haiti without referring to Eddy Bastien and a few other rare exceptions. His vision of the world inspires me, as do his passion for the public interest and, above all, his way of cultivating honesty. Contrary to the majority of politicians who believe that morality and politics are in no way complementary, he believes that we must, at all times and in all places, sanitize and moralize public life. He always told me: *"Daniel, the one who holds the public power, is not a leader or a superman; they are just a simple servant. It is a privilege that we have to be vested with the power to participate in and organize public life. Let us honestly serve the homeland and our compatriots!* »

The miracle of honesty

MY FIRST STEPS TOWARDS FINANCIAL INDEPENDENCE AND THE TEMPTATION TO BE DISHONEST

After my classical studies, I left the city of Port-de-Paix for Port-au-Prince to begin my university studies. Because of the difficulties inherent in student life, I had to start looking for a job. My esteemed childhood friend **Robens MAXI** told me that the NGO where he was active as an executive had just started a recruitment process for the position of Field Coordinator. This job opportunity seemed like an opportunity not to be missed. The year is 2009.

Several young people aspired to obtain the said position. During the job interview, I performed remarkably, even though I was only in my first year of university. However, a brilliant young woman who already had a bachelor's degree in psychology and was doing a master's degree in population and development at the time attracted much more attention from the decision-making panel, which almost unanimously favored her.

One morning, a charming voice called me to tell me I had not been chosen for the job. I reluctantly thanked the lady who called to inform me about the panel's decision. Once I hung up the phone, I prayed, "My God, I know this decision is not yours because you know how much I need this job. I waited for her to call me to tell me it was a mistake. Amen!"

On the first Monday after the fatal phone call, I learned that the young psychologist selected for the position was already

Honesty | Chapitre II

working, and was occupying the office assigned to this function. My faith and conviction remained intact. I remember saying to Robens: this job is mine. I'm waiting for someone to call me to come to work.

Three days later, on Thursday of the same week, the young woman told the office that she did not intend to return because she was far too qualified for the salary she had been offered, US$300.

Robens Maxi, who was in the secret of the gods, rushed to call me and tell me that the young lady had just given up the post and that it would not be long before it would be offered to me. I cannot describe my joy from that day to this day.

A few moments after my friend's anticipation, the same voice that had called me to tell me the bad news said to me that the institution was ready to entrust me with the position if I accepted the monthly salary of three hundred (300) US dollars, the equivalent of twelve thousand (12,000) gourdes. I cheerfully replied that I accepted the proposal and wanted to start work the next day. All excited!

"My God, you have answered my request as I have done it," I said as tears of joy flooded my face.

GO FROM 0 TO 12,000 GOURDES

The US$300 salary this international organization paid me was my first step towards financial self-sufficiency. I saved part of it monthly to build an investment fund to launch my

The miracle of honesty

first business, **"Dal Papeterie."** Some nine months later, it began operating in part of my old folks' home in Port-de-Paix, with my father's consent, **Seldieu Loriston**, and my mother, **Yvanette Joseph.**

At 26, I threw my first stones into the entrepreneurial world. One of the highlights of this company was the printing and photocopying service. I was making a radical change in this area. Thanks to this revolutionary young company's pricing policy, all schools in the North-West department have automatically agreed to present their pupils with typed examination texts. With the presence of Dal Papeterie, the black market in the field of photocopying was banned. As a result of this transformation in the market, persecutions, and mystical "strikes" were the order of the day! Every other morning, there were always signs of fetish activity on the porch of the house where the company was located. It wasn't easy at all!

CONFRONTED WITH DISHONESTY

It took me only a month in my new role as Field Coordinator to discover that some of my co-workers in the office were engaging in dishonest practices and corruption. Their actions were considered normal in their eyes since they were money from an NGO collected from donors. Of course, these were funds offered by donors. Still, the objective was to improve the socio-economic conditions of the program's beneficiaries, who are only our brothers and sisters floundering in poverty and underdevelopment.

Honesty | Chapitre II

One of the activities of this program was to pay for the schooling of beneficiary children in the areas of **Martissant, Fontamara, Bizoton, Thor, Cotes-Plage, Mahotière, Arcachon, Brochette, Waney, Lamentin, Marianie and Carrefour.**

In some cases, some field workers who acted as liaisons between the principals of the community schools and the NGO reached a compromise with some school officials to increase the price of the annual school fees, which were initially generally low. Thus, for a school year whose price was 3000 gourdes, the organization was charged between 10,000 and 15,000 gourdes.

As a newly recruited coordinator, I received from accounting a batch of more than 300 cheques with stubs mentioning the name of the child for whom the cheque had been issued and the name of the school to which the cheque was to be delivered. My work on the cheques was limited to checking whether the number of beneficiary children enrolled in the program corresponded to the number of cheques issued. As a result of the comparison, I had to hand over the cheques to the liaison officers. The latter were responsible for delivering them to the school officials. So, I decided to do more than I had been asked to do.

When I looked at the amount on some of the cheques for community schools, something in me told me that some of the amounts seemed suspicious. How could community schools cost so much? While other private schools in the capital cost about the same amount for a year. Critical Thinking Exercise! While I was doing this work, liaison officers were swarming my office to collect cheques and deliver them to the schools. I asked them to wait a bit while I finished the comparison. Some promised to help me go faster, and others said, "You're new. You haven't mastered your tasks yet." I kept my cool and pretended that, as a newcomer, I wanted to take the time to check everything, so I didn't make any mistakes. Still, their tenacity in getting the checks only increased my suspicions. My conscience would not permit me to cause or sustain dishonest acts. To do so would be renouncing all the moral values I had acquired during my family, religious, and philosophical upbringing.

I decided to lock the checks in my office and ask the driver, willing to take me to a few randomly selected schools, to check the accurate price of school fees. At some distance from the school, I asked the driver to let me walk so as not to let it be understood that I was an employee of the NGO. I make the principals believe that I have just met a destitute child who is not in school and for whom I would like to pay for a school year in exchange for finding the school slip for his class. The reading of the slips threw me into utter indignation.

DISHONEST PEOPLE ARE WILLING TO DO ANYTHING

Once they learned of the audit work with school principals, the liaison officers could not hide their apprehensions and anger. Some would call me to tell me they would decide to

Honesty | Chapitre II

share the surplus with me, even if I had to have 70 percent and they had 30 percent.

They told me I was going against a practice that had been in place for four years. They pointed out that before I joined, my predecessors were happy to adapt to it. My answer was clear: "It would be dishonest of me to take a gourde in addition to the 12,000 gourdes for which I signed my employment contract." One of those liaison officers whose image I still remember, very aggressive, asked me if I wasn't afraid of leaving my skin on a pile of rubbish. He reminded me that he lived in a working-class neighborhood where men were paid to kill people daily. I remember telling him that my parents taught me that it would be better to die than to commit a single dishonest act.

A quote from Socrates I read in my final year of high school reinforced my conviction: *"I consider myself too great to stoop to prove the excellence of my life. I'd rather die than beg for the favor of living."*

It took me a week to finish my cleansing and straightening work. The results were awe-inspiring: I was able to return three (3) million gourdes to the coffers of this NGO without anyone asking me and without wanting to be rewarded. I did it because I knew it was right and in line with honesty. Every time we do something honest, a miracle happens.

GO FROM $300 TO $1000

After a few months in this position, thanks to the accumulated experiences, my Curriculum Vitae became more convincing

The miracle of honesty

and allowed me to get a new job in the NGO sector, but in a more exciting and better-paid position. I went from three hundred (300) to one thousand (1,000) US dollars monthly. This increase in income has dramatically strengthened the performance of my small business. Every month, I invested $700 of my new salary. I firmly believed in supporting my young business and understood that my salary was the primary source of funding for it.

GO FROM $1000 TO $1500

The devastating earthquake of 12 January 2010, which killed more than 300,000 people in a matter of seconds, increased the search for experienced professionals among NGOs capable of working in humanitarian emergencies and hard-to-reach areas. Another NGO recruited me for a new position in an emergency response program and offered me a salary of $1,500. Another increase in income allowed me to strengthen my investments.

I should point out that all this was done in record time, but I did not change my lifestyle. I continued to invest in my small business and saved money to build a medium-term investment fund. Unlike other young people my age who bought gadgets, nice clothes, and other trendy items, I continued to lead the same lifestyle.

In this new position, my responsibilities were greater. I was leading an area development program for World Vision International in the Central Plateau region. An annual budget of **US$900,000** was allocated to this program. I remember how I worked hard to direct the use of these funds towards improving the quality of life of the children in the area. Not a single penny of that amount was misspent. I am proud to have had the privilege of managing such a large amount of money without being tempted to divert a single penny for my benefit or the benefit of anyone else. All these experiences I have had since a young age have exposed me to situations of strong temptations that have strengthened my convictions and commitment to honesty and transparency in management. All my immediate collaborators, accountants, and project managers knew of my purity.

On the day I left World Vision, a festive meeting was organized in my honor and the presence of many other executives of the organization, such as **Evenel MOROSE, Etzer Beaura, Paulaine SAINVAL**, etc., members of community and peasant organizations of Coladère and my supervisors. Emotions ran high when farmers, collaborators, and even those I knew were harshly reprimanded took the floor to declare they had never met a young man so tenacious in transparency and honesty. Some people shed tears of regret when I left. The greatest strength there can be is honesty.

LATEST FULL-TIME WORK EXPERIENCE

In 2012, I moved into a management position. It was also my last step in the NGO sector. This position earned me a fairly significant salary promotion. I went from a salary of 1500 to 3000 US dollars per month, added to that, an operating fee of 15,000 gourdes.

The miracle of honesty

This last salary allowed me to save about 2000 US dollars monthly for at least six months. This requires a certain amount of discipline and financial intelligence: when an ordinary person receives a salary increase, they adjust to a higher lifestyle.

After nine months in this new position, I resigned to return to Port de Paix and devote myself solely to my business ventures. It was a courageous decision that bordered on madness, yet it was a calculated risk and an adventure I have never regretted! I took the time to mention all my salaries, not to show that I was paid well, but to teach young people how I used them effectively and how I went about building a sizeable short-term investment fund. Lower your lifestyle in the present and save money at a constant pace; you will be able to draw a bright future thanks to the increase in your financial intelligence. That's what I do all the time!

THE PATH TO HONESTY IS A HARD FIGHT

In September 2013, I returned to Port-de-Paix, intending to devote myself entirely to entrepreneurship. The year before, having had the privilege of visiting Canada, I saw an amazing restaurant there. From that day on, I said to myself: "When I have the means, I will offer a restaurant of this quality to the city where I grew up." Thanks to the considerable savings I could make from my last salaries, I had more than 80% of the amount I had to invest to carry out this project (to establish a standard restaurant of international quality).

Honesty | Chapitre II

A few months later, I started my 2nd business called Dal Restaurant. It was an investment of several million gourdes. To complete this project, I had to resort to Micro-Crédit National, a subsidiary of UNIBANK, for a loan of 800,000 gourdes because I didn't have enough cash on hand.

The Dal Restaurant concept was revolutionary. A restaurant that the city was going to see for the first time. It was a luxury restaurant in a dusty town. In such a short time, it has attracted more than 95% of visitors (official and international delegations) and more than 80% of the area's people. One of the innovations of this concept was a buffet that offered a variety of dishes and spared the customer the burden of waiting up to 45 minutes for the dish ordered by other traditional restaurants, regardless of the level of hunger or eagerness. With the Dal Restaurant concept, the customer began to enjoy his dish of choice kept warm in a heated display case using the **"bain marie method"** just after placing his order.

In its first week of launch, Dal restaurant was a dazzling success. This was due to the technologies used there and the equipment of international standards that increased its rapid and massive production capacity.

The consumption room was similar to a playground every lunchtime for public and private institutions in the area. My wife and I had put all our soul and youthful passion into this project to serve our customers the difference in the form of dishes.

| The miracle of honesty

While Dal Restaurant was a great success from the moment it launched, thanks to the innovation it brought, it also shook up other traditional restaurants established years before it. We didn't realize it, but the other restaurants were closed. Most customers left for Dal Restaurant when the need to eat arose. Instead of taking the initiative to level up (which would benefit consumers), some restaurant owners decided to act in Haitian-style. A mystical battle was being waged against Dal Restaurant.

THE POWER OF HAITIAN WITCHCRAFT IN DESTRUCTION

One day, one of these restaurant owners came to visit us. Sat down while admiring Dal Restaurant's wooden tables and straw chairs made by the hands of Haitian artisans. Bought a Coca-Cola before saying goodbye to us. This man had not really come to consume but was in possession of a "mystical charge" commonly called in the witchcraft language **"expedition."** This consisted of placing a demon (Baka) at each end of the restaurant's front door. The positioning of these evil spirits at the front door was strategic. These demons were tasked with closing the main door of the restaurant.

You may be wondering; how can a mind close a door that is physical matter? You are right to ask yourself such a question! But don't forget that the mind can project itself onto matter! These spiritual entities (the BAKA), creations of man, have a high level of power and carry out the orders they receive from initiates or voodoo priests with almost flawless precision. The two (2) demons I'm talking about here have been instructed

| 69

Honesty | Chapitre II

to exert a kind of hypnosis on every person approaching the restaurant to come to consume and to make them see the door closed while it is still wide open.

One of my employees told me that one day, when he was standing at the restaurant's front door, he saw a man arrive as he was about to enter. With a blink, the potential customer stopped in front of the door and said:
-Why is Dal restaurant closing so early today?
Unaware of what was going on, the employee replied:
"Sir, if the door is open, why do you imagine we are not working?"

The hypnotized customer replied, *"But the door was closed when I arrived. You've probably just opened it to call me.*

So far, no one has understood anything. My employee told me the story as the joke of the day. As if the gentleman was stricken with myopia or some kind of visual weakness. This is also the same conclusion that I have made. I couldn't even relate the considerable drop in the number of customers we knew we were receiving before to the behavior of those hypnotized customers who turned back because they understood that the door of Dal restaurant (even though it was wide open) was closed. A stroke of genius...

During this period, when the Baka performed their duties brilliantly, the restaurant endured considerable deficits on a daily basis. It became an empire that collapsed before the helpless eyes of its supporters.

The miracle of honesty

HOW DID WE KNOW WHAT WAS GOING ON?

While passing through the city of Port of Peace, a man who lived in the United States arrived at the restaurant: a friend had advised him to trust Dal restaurant to feed himself during his stay. This gentleman, it seems, was an initiate, if not a connoisseur, in the mystical field. He was greeted by my wife, who managed our catering establishment. Having sensed the presence of the demons (BAKA), he would sit down and murmur:

OH MY GOD! MEN ARE WICKED.

"Is the owner of this restaurant a child?" he asked my wife, whom he took to be a mere clerk. Could you allow me to speak to the owner? He insisted.

"You can talk to me. I'm his wife, and I'm the one who manages the restaurant," retorted **Marie Priscile Royaque Loriston**.

"Madam, someone has closed your restaurant and placed two BAKAs at both front door ends. I managed to get in because I'm not a layman. But strong hypnosis is exerted on every person who approaches your restaurant by making them see the door closed. "If you don't mind, I can hunt them for you and send them back to the person who sent them," said the customer, who seemed to have mastered some mystical knowledge.

"I am a Mormon Christian and cannot make this commitment without my husband's approval. Let me call him," added Priscile.

That day, I received a call from my wife telling me that a character wanted to talk to me about such an important subject. I scrambled to the restaurant while the curious

| 71

Honesty | Chapitre II

customer enjoyed his dish with appetite and devoured the supple flesh of the goat dish he had ordered.

When I arrived at the restaurant, the mysterious customer said to me:

"Mr. Loriston, I know you are a Christian, but your restaurant has a problem whose solution must not wait. I can drive out the BAKA (demons) placed here with a simple method and words of power. What I will have to do to help you is not a snag in your religious faith. It's just knowledge like any other that I'll exercise, and I'll only need salt and a little hot water!

To convince me, he goes one step further:

-If you find that I am making a gesture similar to a ritual contrary to your Christian faith during my performance, feel free to ask me to quickly stop what I am doing. And I will obey! Mr. Loriston, put a saucepan filled with water on a stove until it comes to a boil, and then, while it boils, give me a good amount of salt. Do you see, Mr. Loriston? It's that simple!

Once boiled, I gave the gentleman the water with a good quantity of salt. He took the salt and sent a portion of it to each end of the front door, saying, "Get out of this space and go back to the one who brought you here!" He uttered other words I couldn't hear but were "words of power" to repeat.

During that same week, the restaurant regained its splendor, and the employees began to smile again. Customers automatically came back and started queuing again. Demand once again outstripped supply!

A SECOND "STRIKE."

A few weeks passed. The people who had prepared the BAKA coup understood that the BAKA had been driven out and that they had no negative influence on Dal Restaurant.

> **The miracle of honesty**

They decided to strike another blow. This time, it was an "expedition" in the form of a foul smell that permeated the dining room. This unpleasant exhalation was not present in the toilets, the kitchen, or the small warehouse where the restaurant's stock was kept. She was only stuck in the room set up to receive customers.

We first thought that a rat might be dead somewhere and decomposing. In the meantime, in search of a possible cause of this disturbing smell, we temporarily closed the restaurant to move all the equipment and furniture. A week later, the search proved useless and unsuccessful...

One morning, I was weeping profusely as I prayed fervently to God, *"My God if the money I have invested in this restaurant is the fruit of my fairly earned salaries, if I have committed no act of corruption or dishonesty to gather these investment funds, why do you let dishonest and backward people do all this to me?"*

As I ended my prayer in which I seemed to be blaming God, it occurred to me to do a Google search. I soon realized that it was a prompting of the spirit and an immediate answer to my prayer. I eagerly went to this search engine to write the following sentence: *"How do you get rid of a bad smell naturally?"*

GOD CAN USE ALL MAN-MADE TOOLS TO WORK MIRACLES

My Google search found a variety of answers. I chose the simplest one since I could see the natural ingredients and materials she mentioned: coffee powder, a boiler, and a stove.

Honesty | Chapitre II

I did as the answer to my search dictated. I bought powdered coffee, put it in a bucket on a stove in the center of the house, and stirred the coffee with a wooden spoon so that it would fill the room. As the smell of roasted coffee spread, the foul smell gradually diminished until it disappeared entirely and permanently.

Finally, after a week of sudden closure for a reason that customers could not have known, after many deficits recorded, Dal restaurant reopened its doors. But all these evil assaults were not without consequences. They automatically demobilized part of the clientele, constituted a loss of financial income, and only weakened the young company, which was worth millions of gourdes in equipment.

The restaurant continued to operate after these unfair actions, but it was no longer solvent. He could not bring in the 68,000 gourdes (capital and interest) required by the loan contract of UNIBANK's microfinance service, MCN, per month—three consecutive months without being able to make a single full payment. The pressures were mounting. MCN's debt collectors had become threatening. They acted like the savage robots of an animal-faced capitalist system. Suddenly, the enthusiastic, responsible, honest young man who respected his commitments that I was projected the image of a non-solvent citizen.

BE HONEST AT ALL TIMES

I will never forget that gloomy morning when I received a delegation of two local debt collectors and a regional manager. This encounter, which took place inside the

The miracle of honesty

restaurant, was the most remarkable moment of pressure I have ever experienced in my entire life. The bank was about to set in motion a process that could tarnish my reputation and make me look like a defaulter. My whole soul and my wife's soul were swallowed up. I left the discussion table with tears in my eyes legs shaking. I had no hope or any other source where I could find some money to pay into the bank to calm their harshness.

Five minutes after the bank representatives had left the restaurant, a purchasing manager from one of the departmental offices of the public administration entered the room and asked to see me. He needed a receipt for six hundred thousand gourdes (600,000 gourdes) showing that I had offered a catering service. Then he would bring me the check on the condition that I agree to give him 50% of the check amount and keep the other 50% for the restaurant.

At first glance, it seemed like a miracle, a response to all the pressure I had just been under from the bank officials. They pressed me for three times sixty-eight thousand gourdes, and this gentleman came to offer me three times a hundred thousand gourdes for a simple sealed receipt. I looked into the eyes of my interlocutor and said: *"Unfortunately, I can't do this. It will be an act of corruption!"* Embarrassed, he moved without saying a word.

It is necessary to have a firm conviction and a perfect knowledge of what honesty is in order not to succumb to

Honesty | Chapitre II

these circumstances of great temptation. Dishonesty will never be the way offered by either God or nature! "If you're going to get out of this situation, it has to be with dignity," said a voice inside me.

My wife looked me in the eye and said, "Honey, I'm proud of you. I love the man you are! We'd kiss, and we'd start crying. We wept for two reasons: first, because we had acted honestly; secondly, because, at the same time, we remembered that we had no hope of finding the means to pay the bank.

A week passed. We were not yet able to find a more or less significant sum to show the bank our willingness to extinguish the debt. I decided to go to Port-au-Prince to meet some friends and former co-workers, to explain my situation, and to see to what extent they could lend me money to pay the bank, even if it were just a full payment while I waited for me to find a way out or a strategy to rectify the situation.

I leave the city of Port de Paix at six (6) o'clock in the morning. I'm alone in the car, holding the steering wheel with the strength of a baby a few months old. I'm devastated. Stressed and pensive. At times, comforting songs come to mind, but sad thoughts always take over. I continue on the road to Port-au-Prince like a shy and unconfident driver.

As I leave the **TiTanyen area**, my phone rings. At the other end of the line was a man's voice, an employee of the central office of Micro-Crédit National.

The miracle of honesty

"Mr. Loriston!" We are about to send the newspaper Le Nouvelliste a list of bad payers. Unfortunately, sir, your name is on the list. My whole soul had flown away. I suddenly become flabbergasted. A long silence was pierced by the roaring sound of the vehicle's engine.

- Hello, Hello, Hello, are you on the line Mr. Loriston?

I answer with determination:

"Sir, I am on my way to Port-au-Prince; please remove my name from this list! I am a 31-year-old. I have a whole future ahead of me. I am in a difficult situation, but this debt is close to my heart. Before I finish, the bank employee replies:

"Mr. Loriston!" If you can promise me to make a payment of 68,000 gourdes before 2 o'clock this very day, I will immediately strike your name off the list that is going to be published.

To save time and give him confidence, I tell him:

- I've just left "**Titanyen**" area. I'm in the vicinity of **Source Puante**. What is the nearest UNIBANK branch?

- The Lathan branch in the **Bon Repos** area, which should normally be less than 15 minutes away from where you are now, the employee points out.

"Remove my name from this list. I'll go to the Lathan branch."

I didn't really know what I was going to do. I parked the car on the side of the road to think. The image of a friend whom I had helped many times to find work in the various NGOs for which I worked came to mind. I quickly called to tell him I was in an extreme emergency and had to find 68,000 gourdes immediately. This friend had only 800 US dollars, the equivalent of 48,000 gourdes, in his account. I told him to deposit the $800 into my account at UNIBANK quickly.

Honesty | Chapitre II

I felt relieved when he returned the call to tell me he had just made the deposit. I figured that with a deposit of 48,000 gourdes; I would be more convincing: I was determined to ask them to allow me to pay the remaining 20,000 gourdes the next day.

With the utmost eagerness, I went to the Lathan branch. As soon as I arrived, I took the line and waited my turn to be served. My heart was in distress. it was bearing the brunt of my stress. It was beating at an explosive rate. Thinking that the deposit I was going to make would not be a full payment made me lose confidence in myself. Suddenly, the cashier, a tall young man wearing a white shirt and blue tie, rang the bell and asked me to come closer to his till.

-What is the exchange rate today? I asked!

"60 gourdes to a U.S. dollar," he replied.

"Okay, I'd like to exchange 800 dollars!"

The cashier took the $800 and tested it with a small machine. Then he counted them and cashed them in. He took the exchange card and wrote down the amount of 48,000 gourdes. He rang his bell to receive another customer after asking me to stand next to check the count. A few minutes later, I noticed that I had at my disposal the 20,000 gourdes I needed to make a full payment. I realized that the cashier had just made a colossal mistake.

I returned to him to tell him that he gave me 68,000 gourdes instead of 48,000.

"Sir, I gave you precisely the amount of your $800.

I insisted:

The miracle of honesty

"Sir, you have given me a considerable surplus!"
"Let me do my work." I checked your money twice before handing it over to you. The amount is accurate! The cashier chanted nervously.

In the meantime, the branch supervisor, who was not too far away, heard my voice and approached me to ask for an explanation. I explained that the cashier refused to receive the 20,000 gourdes he had inadvertently given me. Surprised by my behavior, the supervisor invited me into his office to verify the transaction better. Having noticed that the amount I had just been given was more than what I was entitled to, the supervisor did not hide his astonishment.
-Who are you? he asked.
"I am a young man in great difficulty, pressured by Unibank's microfinance for a loan in arrears, but who decides to keep his honesty intact in all circumstances," I replied.
As I told him this, tears fell from my eyes. He knew something was wrong. He wanted more details.

It was then that I explained to him the situation and the pressures that the MCN was putting on me. I told him that despite everything, I refused to take advantage of this mistake on the teller's part to pay the bank a full payment. Impressed by my firmness and deep moral conviction, the supervisor picked up the phone to speak to MCN officials at the central office in Port-au-Prince. He explained to them what had just happened and asked them to consider the rare loyalty I displayed. So, he suggested they reschedule the loan for me and let me pay monthly according to my income. The central office welcomed his proposal, and all the pressures fell that day!

Isn't this a mighty miracle of honesty? Yes!

Back in Port-de-Paix, my wife and I decided to close the restaurant and sell all the equipment we had to pay off part of the debt. On the other hand, we continued to make monthly payments on the debt from the meager income our first business generated. Dal Papeterie paid a good part of a debt that had not been contracted for its purpose.

TESTING AS A SOURCE OF LEARNING

Two years after the total closure of Dal restaurant, I couldn't get rid of the desire to be successful in the restaurant business. So, I launched a new concept called Wifi bar. It was a snack bar offering sandwiches, pancakes, pizzas, hamburgers, and drinks, especially to schoolchildren and students of Port de Paix who needed a quiet space with a Wifi connection to do their homework. But the general population had access to it.

All you had to do was pay for a bottle of water to be connected to the WIFI of this snack bar and start doing your research on the net. At that time, public WIFI connections were rare in the city. The concept was new. He drew the crowd in again. It was the first catering service of its kind in the area. Everywhere we went, people were praising this innovation. This time, the competition was less fierce since Wifi bar offered exclusive products and was aiming for a market share that did not exist before.

The miracle of honesty

A few months later, a socio-economic crisis due to political instability caused the already very low purchasing power of the population of the North-West to fall, which had severe consequences for the profitability of the initiative. Once again, this second attempt to exploit a significant market share in the restaurant sector failed. This several thousand US dollars investment flowed like a straw castle, making me wade in deep pain. There were still things to learn!

In the meantime, I continued to travel to countries such as the Dominican Republic, the Bahamas, and the United States of America. Thus, I saw the opportunity that mass restoration offers. I persisted in believing that I could make a lot of money in this field (catering), which fascinates me so much.

A SIMPLE READING MADE ME UNDERSTAND EVERYTHING

After this second failed attempt, I offered to get more books on entrepreneurship, marketing, management, economics, and financial intelligence to strengthen my knowledge in these areas. I bought one of Robert Kiyosaki's books, *"Develop Your Financial Intelligence."* While reading this book, I came across the following sentence that multiplied my intelligence by ten (10): "Look at what the people around you like; offer it to them."

Before, I didn't always pay attention to what people liked, and I always offered them what I enjoyed myself and what flattered my greatness. That's when I realized that my second failure in the restaurant business was because I decided to offer what I liked instead of what was wanted.

Honesty | Chapitre II

As soon as I discovered this, I started looking for a concept in the restaurant industry that would allow me to meet what people want. I persisted in believing I could create a niche in the restaurant market and make up for all the time I later lost in this field. I was overwhelmed by a kind of rage to win and the desire to achieve exceptional results in this field that I am so passionate about.

SOMETHING CLICKED IN DECEMBER 2020

In December 2020, during the patron saint festivities of the city of Port de Paix, the late President Jovenel Moise announced that the national carnival would take place there in February 2021. If, when this news was announced, some saw well-decorated musical floats and the usual decibel war in their imagination, I saw it as an opportunity to launch a mass catering service with an unparalleled commercial production capacity. I told myself that if tens of thousands of people take to the streets of the city for three (3) days, there will not be a supply proportional to the demand for food.

In the same week, I embarked on a trip to the United States of America to purchase catering equipment with a highly commercial production capacity: Automatic juice dispensers, industrial fryers, BBQ machines, crêpe makers, etc.

I've bought almost all the equipment that American fast-food restaurants use. Undoubtedly, I have the highest production capacity of all the catering establishments in the area.

The miracle of honesty

Unfortunately, like all other cities, the carnival organization had a purely political aspect. As the days went by, I did not receive any contract from the Town Hall, the local committee, or any state institution on site, despite all the photos of materials, promotional leaflets, and copies of the patent I had submitted. I was not a supporter of the powers that be. No matter what taxes I paid in the commune or how many jobs I created, I had no right to lend my services to the small part of the Haitian State transferred to Port-de-Paix by the late memory of His Excellency President **Jovenel Moïse**. Yet, ordinary citizens with no restaurant, no license, and no talent in the culinary arts had very juicy restaurant contracts. Everything was done as if it were not a state activity financed by the public treasury. There was a total lack of transparency in organizing one of the world's largest festival. Two years later, there has been no report on the budget allocated or the expenditure made, and silence and secrecy continue! The principle of accountability has once again been flouted without the slightest embarrassment.

Nature always makes amends for injustices. Two days before the carnival festivities, I received two calls from Port-au-Prince: one from **Patrick Moussignac**, the general manager of Radio Caraïbes Fm, and the other from a former co-worker. Mr. Patrick Moussignac entrusted me with the catering of the plethora of staff of Radio Télé Caraïbes, who ensured the broadcasting of the festivities. My former colleague asked me to hire my services from the Ministry of Health: they were looking for a restaurant that could offer a quality service.

Honesty | Chapitre II

As soon as the price of the services was concluded, I mobilized my entire team and all the necessary logistics. In addition, I recruited fifteen new people for temporary employment. The news of the services I offered went around the city. Other ministerial delegations came to share the delicious dishes prepared for the benefit of the Ministry of Health. The difference is noticeable, they said. It was a hard blow to the obscurantists of **Jovenel's power** in Port-de-Paix, who aspired to punish me for my outspokenness, my difficult positions on matters of public interest, and the relevance of my criticism of the corrupt public authorities in Haiti.

If it weren't for my connections in Port-au-Prince, the thousands of US dollars I invested to acquire high-end equipment would be a miscalculation. Mother Nature never lets a good, caring, honest heart suffers the wickedness of the mediocre. The two contracts I found allowed me to earn a more or less considerable sum!

In addition, I decided to launch a new restaurant concept in the North-West based on the materials I had bought for the organization of the national carnival in Port-de-Paix. Although I was missing the forecasts, I had made regarding possible receipts linked to the sales that the carnival would have caused, I wondered how I could use these materials in the long term to attract a significant market share. I didn't want the boycott I suffered to quench my flame and passion for catering.

This is how I came to mind the image of the small street food restaurants I saw in Manhattan during a tourist trip to

The miracle of honesty

New York State. After much thinking and studying, I realized there would be many opportunities if I launched a street food restaurant that would symbolize luxury or modernity right on the ground and at unbeatable prices.

Under a tent set up in a non-concrete space, i.e., dusty, measuring 10 meters by 10 meters, I placed the same equipment the big American fast-food restaurants used. This created euphoria, an attraction that traditional marketing could not provoke. From day one, customers were pouring in. The staff was overwhelmed. We were selling like none of my companies had ever done before!

EVERYTHING EXISTS FROM ITS OPPOSITE

I use this philosophical maxim to explain that there is always the option of a glorious opportunity behind any unfortunate situation. To put it better, you can turn a problematic situation into an opportunity. My experience with Jovenel Moise's henchmen is a vivid illustration of this. For example, in this book, you read about my persecution. Indeed, some people have tried to smear my reputation as an honest man.

Even today, a machine of defamation is set in motion to smear my reputation for an act that two other civilly and criminally liable have committed (the Bank Pa Nou case). These people, who always feel annoyed because I apologize for honesty in my public speeches daily, want to take advantage of the laziness that haunts social networks to invent a digital version of a Daniel Loriston who would be dishonest. Instead of lamenting,

Honesty | Chapitre II

I am taking advantage of this situation to build a new phase of my reputation as a man jealously attached to his unshakable loyal convictions by writing a book devoted solely to the notion of honesty. In addition to being a young man whose honesty has never wavered, I am one of the few Haitian authors to devote their time and thoughts to this concept.

BEING HONEST ALSO MEANS PAYING A FULL TITHE

One of the sacred laws taught in the Bible, and one of the principles clearly taught in the vast and rigorous Mormon doctrine, is the law of tithing. This law stipulates that one must give one-tenth of all one's income to the lord. Hebrews 7:1–10; Genesis 14:19–20; 28:20-22 say a little about this commandment. From my childhood, my parents, who are faithful Mormons taught me this law as an opportunity to show or show gratitude to God for the blessings received.

As a child, I took pleasure in paying tithing by giving away some of the pennies I received from my parents. Of all the commands that Christianity teaches in general, this seems to me to be the most difficult to observe since one must pay to keep it. Yet, it hides a secret and a powerful promise that many people miss. This promise and secret is elucidated in Malachi 3:10: *"Bring all the tithes to the treasure house, that there may be food in my house; "Put me to the test," declares the LORD Almighty. And you will see if I do not open the windows of heaven for you, if I do not pour out blessings upon you in abundance."*

The miracle of honesty

Even outside of the religious context, I find it appropriate to share a little of what we have, help each other, and support the poor and needy.

I paid a faithful title on the earnings of the small business, as with all my other businesses. I testify that alongside all the intelligence I apply in the management of my activities, all my entrepreneurial creativity, and all the good services I offer, the law of tithing is a pillar in the success of this restaurant concept.

The abundant blessing in the above-mentioned text cannot be understood only as the acquisition of material things such as money or goods. It should also be understood as the set of new ideas that have helped me improve the quality of services. It is also every action that has been dictated to me during my reflections in order to be able to make this initiative more competitive and profitable. It was also the good employees I was able to recruit and the unfortunate incidents we were able to neutralize in time. Better than anyone, I have a vast and unfathomable testimony of the power and immediacy of the blessings of the law of tithing. If nothing is true, let us spare the law of tithing.

Thanks to the many blessings poured on this daring initiative, the concept I boldly call in the Creole language, KWEN DAL (Dal's Corner), has undergone a metamorphosis of rare significance. Sales were exploding at an unexpectedly high rate. As a result, six months later, I could afford a mobile food kiosk to replace the small canvas tent used to protect the physical facilities.

Nine months later, we established another outlet specializing in selling sandwiches. With this decision, I was looking to diversify the distribution channel of the small business and, at the same time, expand the customer base. Finally, I brought a restaurant on wheels, a food truck, to Haiti. It is the first electric car to set foot on Haitian soil.

Do you see how a boycott has served as an extraordinary source of blessings? The marriage of honesty and intelligence can transform the worst of all worlds, transcend people's lives, and significantly improve their lives.

BOILER PÂTÉ: EQUILIBRIUM PRICE

This experience with KWENDAL Street Food allowed me to understand the effects of mass production and the strength of pricing policy when you want to increase your market share. She also taught me you must follow sales trends to invest your funds well.

During a strategic meeting to find a mass-market product at a meager price, our chef (catering professional) Besty Bière Michou Jean Baptiste, an extraordinary young girl who had come from Port-au-Prince to support the local staff, offered me the **"pâté-chaudière (Boiler pâté)."** This type of pâté is also called **"paté kòde"** in Haitian cuisine.

The miracle of honesty

I agreed to try Betsy's proposal since most Haitians cherish the pâté and will sell for only 50 gourdes or 0.33 US dollars. Traditional restaurants offered no consumer product to a population that had no real purchasing power at such a price. I thought it could meet a need and immediately create a niche that has been under-exploited until then.

From the first day of the launch of this product, we sold the entire amount produced in the blink of an eye. We tripled the amount the next day, but unfortunately, the supply was less than the demand. This clue quickly taught me that I needed to invest in new equipment to increase supplies and make pâté production a service independent of the rest of the small business.

At the beginning of the year, I obtained a financial loan of 4 million gourdes from **"Koperativ Pou Lespwa"** (**KOPLES**), which I invested in the acquisition of stock. But I couldn't find another loan from the same cooperative to purchase the equipment. While I was wondering where to find these new funds to equip Kwendal properly, the Minister of Commerce **Ricardin Saint-Jean**, an old friend, like me from the city of Saint Louis du Nord, was taking part in the festivities of Saint Louis du Nord. He took the opportunity to go to Kwendal with the entire ministerial delegation and buy food.

When the Minister of Trade and Industry arrived, he noticed the long queue and the number of young people working under my supervision. So, he understood that my greatest passion was to help the Northwest see the light at the end of the tunnel.

"You need funding, Daniel," he said. FDI, the Industrial Development Fund, makes up to 2 million gourdes available to small businesses. You can apply yourself, and I will tell the officials that you are impacting the job market in the Northwest and that you are well qualified for such a loan. But we won't give you the cash; we'll pay for the materials you need.

Thus, three months later, after receiving all the legal and administrative proofs, the FDI issued a cheque for 2 million gourdes in the name of a shop in Pétion Ville that was responsible for providing me with the materials I needed to increase the production of pâté. A loan that I started to repay after three months of grace.

Launching this new project has significantly improved my vision as an entrepreneur and has impacted the lives of an entire population. The pâté production plant has created 100 new permanent jobs in Port-de-Paix alone. This massive production workshop operates 24 hours a day. Three groups of employees working in rotation every 8 hours produce 4,000 pies daily.

More than sixty street vendors scattered in the different streets and neighborhoods of the city bring the small "pâté-chauds" to the door of customers who call them as they pass, to the intimacy of the public or private offices where the city's socio-professionals work and on all the playgrounds of schools.

> The miracle of honesty

WE CAN ACHIEVE OUR MOST AMBITIOUS DREAMS BY FOLLOWING THE PATH OF HONESTY

Unfortunately, many people are lured by the ease that leads almost unequivocally to dishonesty and corruption. This often happens to people who want to reach a level of wealth or well-being without knowing how to impose the necessary patience and constant effort on themselves. They are unable to identify the lines that should not be crossed; they do not pass up the accessible opportunities related to corruption that quite often present themselves in the form of opportunities. Yet, no one must take clumsy, circuitous paths to achieve loyal goals.

When I launched this project to produce pâtés on a large scale, some people with complexes saw a reduction in my height in this approach. Still, this sales line alone was helping me earn some pretty significant income. The small table below will give you an idea of the break-even point of this modest initiative in a single month:

Production/day	Price/unit	Sale/day	Sale/week	Sale/ month
4,000 unités	50.00 HTG	200,000 HTG	1,200,000 HTG	4,800,000 HTG

After the salaries paid and the expenses incurred to cover the factors of production, there was still a reasonably satisfactory profit margin that helped me to settle in record time part of the costs of building a dream house in the locality of Aubert, a paradisiacal suburb of the municipality of Port-de-Paix. I bless the name of the Supreme Intelligence and take pride in achieving such feats without recurring corruption.

Honesty | Chapitre II

At the beginning of the launch of this project, I had never imagined that I could collect about 5 million gourdes per month from the sale of pâté-chaudière, an initiative long abandoned to the sole hands of small merchants using rudimentary means who could only produce one or two hundred per day!

The opportunities are numerous, and they are in the details that we neglect. Let's open our eyes, let us have loyalty as our compass, and use our intelligence to move forward toward our dreams and goals. The dishonesty or corruption that causes most of the world's ills is not a viable or feasible option. The latter distorts our humanity and makes us lose sight of the right path and sacred destinies. It never ceases to plunge the world into disarray, into dark pangs. It makes the world ugly and wounds the eyes of the soul.

HOLDING THE BAR FOR HONESTY

We live in an unhinged world. The oldest values, which are most deeply rooted in the constitution of humanity, are crumbling and disappearing at the same rate as civilizational progress. Everything seems to change before our eyes before we have time to catch a glimpse of it. If science could paint a picture of today's world and present it to our ancestors who died a few decades ago, our world would be unrecognizable to them.

But despite all this, we must constantly remind ourselves that honesty is an immutable principle. To think of this virtue is simultaneously recognizing that we must establish

The miracle of honesty

in our life a list of prohibitions, a list of actions that we will never commit under any circumstances. We can live a life of abundance, obtain great wealth, realize great dreams and projects, and live an acceptable life without resorting to disloyal actions.

Despite the significant changes that the world is experiencing, dishonesty is and will remain an unacceptable shortcut. The more the world changes, the better we must hold the integrity bar!

PROMOTING A CULTURE OF HONESTY

Looking at the enormous progress of new information and communication technologies, one wonders why communication and information channels profusely propagate the excesses and defects of the modern world and give little, if any, space to promoting virtues such as honesty and loyalty. Why is the picture of the man who is convicted of rape featured on the front pages of newspapers, while the man who is a responsible family man leading a good life has gone incognito? The media is missing the opportunity to promote the essential values that can turn the world around in its event-driven decline. Schools, universities, government actors, religious assemblies, associations of all kinds, families, and citizens must begin promoting honesty. Let us make the concept of honesty, not a subject that astonishes because of its rarity but an everyday subject. Let us leave the legacy of honesty to future generations, the virtue that is most lacking in today's world.

Honesty | Chapitre II

I remain committed to the idea that if the various governments of the world, civil society organizations, families, social groups, the media, and educational centers make this virtue a value to be instilled in citizens, we can straighten out the world and make it a space where harmony will not be the exception, but rather the rule.

CHAPITRE III

Neutrality in the face of injustice does not exist

"The neutrality in the face of injustice does not exist."

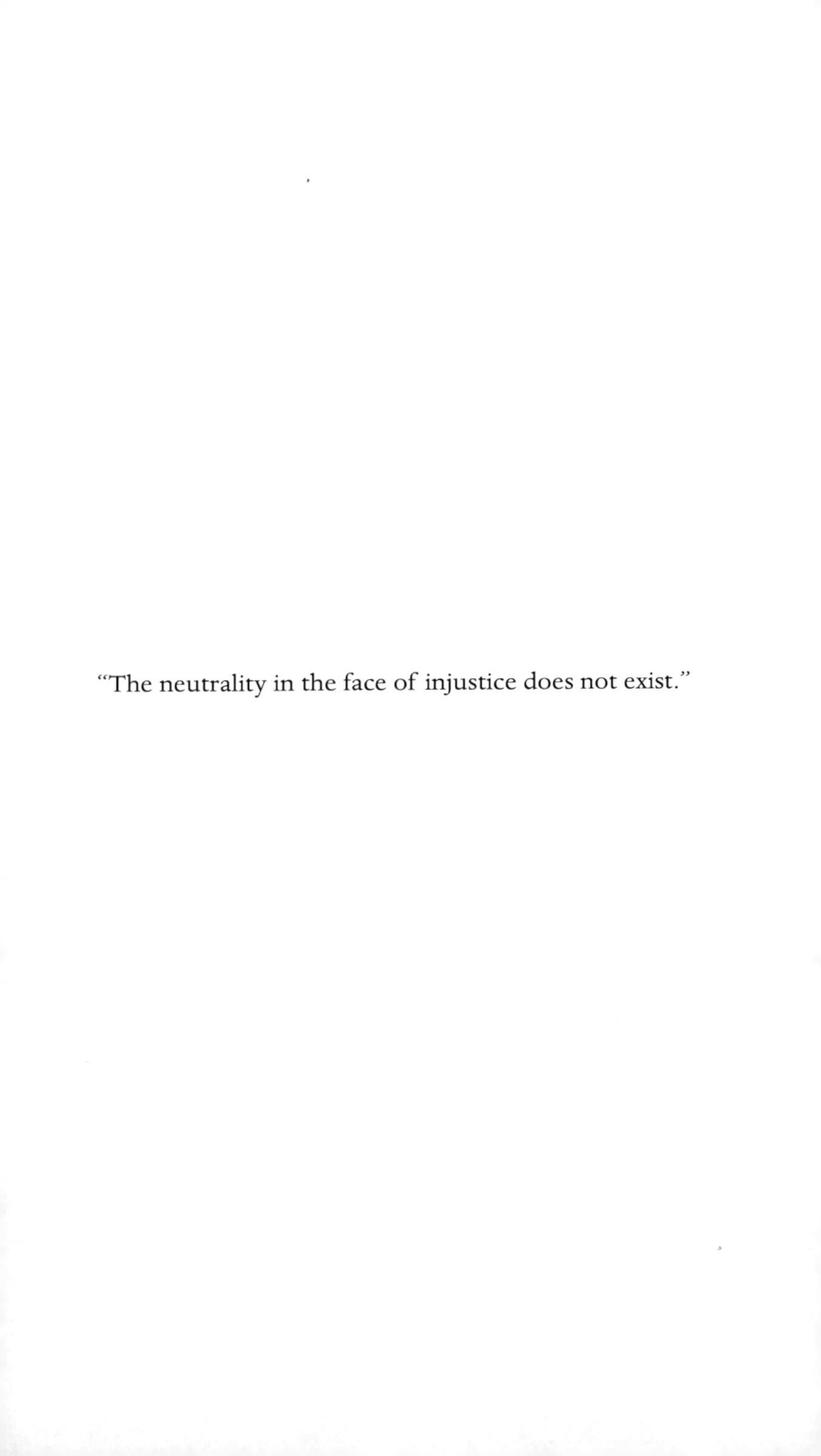

"Neutrality aids the oppressor, never the victim. Silence encourages the tormentor, never the innocent."
Elie Wiesel

"If you are neutral in a situation of injustice, then you have chosen the oppressor's side."
Desmond Tutu

"I understood it was not enough to denounce injustice; you had to give your life to fight it."
Albert CAMUS

"An injustice must not be forgotten or forgiven: Whenever an injustice is committed in the world, somewhere men become worse through discouragement."
Henry de Montherlant

The miracle of honesty

LET US LOVE TRUTH AND JUSTICE

Many thinkers understand **"honesty"** as the character of one who speaks the truth, is outspoken, is sincere in his words, and expresses himself without trying to distort the truth under any circumstances. Admittedly, the concept encompasses a broader meaning, as we have seen in previous chapters, but we approach it here in this chapter from this narrow-angle.

A lack of will plagues humanity. Governments do not tell their constituents the whole truth; Parents, for one reason or another, in many ways, don't tell their children the truth. Paradoxically, we live in an era where we have real-time access to a wide range of information while we swim in a civilization of withholding the truth. In most humans, these and many other attitudes unconsciously develop a refusal to honor the truth.

Neutrality in the face of injustice does not exist | Chapitre III

How many people are chosen as witnesses in court who, after having promised an oath to tell the truth and nothing but the truth, begin to lie as soon as they make the first statements? People who witness a murder, who have all the details about the murderer, and who, despite the tears, the emotion, and the grief of the bereaved families, decide not to tell the truth!

How many times are we slandered and defamed by the general public when one, two, or 40 people know the truth and decide to remain silent? How often are we unfairly accused when our friends, co-workers, or family refuse to tell the truth? Why do these people who know the truth and know how much the enunciation of that truth would be enough to restore our honor, reputation, and fame decide to keep quiet? What an injustice! What a level of human incompetence! What paralysis of the soul! And what an anesthesia of consciousness! I know the depth of the wounds of people who have been slandered and who are unable to restore their honor because witnesses who know the whole truth choose to remain silent and, at the same time, condemn the population to opine according to the lies of the slanderers.

To love the truth means, in my humble opinion, to speak the truth because one cannot bear to have its opposite replace it. It also means that one abhors falsehood so much that one dispels it without hesitation because under no circumstances can a brain that does not suffer from any deformity tolerate for a moment that this vice should take the place of truth. To set the record straight even when the lie seems more popular,

The miracle of honesty

widespread, more believable, and more acceptable is to show an unfailing love for justice, to eject the thick darkness from the throne reserved for the virtue of truth.

We must love the truth even if it is against our interests. To do otherwise is a violation of the rules of nature.

As part of the battle to strengthen the love of truth that is sorely lacking in today's world, I invite parents around the world to follow the counsel of the leader of **The Church of Jesus Christ of Latter-day Saints (Mormon)** to **"teach by example."** If we want our children, for whom we are primarily responsible, to love the truth, we must be the first to cultivate this love for the truth. We are the first heroes that our children will learn to imitate in every detail.

Let us teach children and youth the importance of truth. Let us teach them the value of such virtue and its importance in the race for loyalty, which assures the soul's emancipation and its qualification to unheard-of degrees of glory. Tell them that the truth is at the service of all humanity!

I highly appreciate this quote from the Indian philosopher Swami Vivekananda, born in 1863: *"Man does not progress from error to truth, but from truth to truth, from a lesser truth to a greater truth."* By this thought, the author seems to insinuate that we must not start from error to truth but from truth to itself as a condition closely connected with man's progress. To love the truth is to want to progress.

Neutrality in the face of injustice does not exist | Chapitre III

THE TRUTH IS EXPENSIVE

In our world, truth is a scarce commodity. That's why it's so expensive. Suppose you have never faced a situation of confusion, doubt, or false allegations weighing on your back your reputation. In that case, you cannot understand why I invite my Haitian sisters and brothers to tell the truth. I have more than once been in a situation where only the truth could soothe my sorrow and pains and dispel the doubts that hung over me. Instead of telling the truth, I relied on witnesses who kept silent. In these situations, one is always willing to pay a fortune to make the truth shine. Sadly, blinded by hatred and jealousy, those who should be fulfilling their responsibilities as honest citizens by braving all dangers to honor the truth. Those who sometimes pretend to be people of integrity choose the path of betrayal instead of overturning the lie to light the flame of truth.

Whoever needs the truth to be established in order to wash away his fame will sooner or later receive a great gift: the reparation of his wounded honor. Whoever refuses to tell the truth he knows receives nothing in return. Yet, it persists! If truth is becoming so rare, it is because lies and illusions are on every street corner.

Having suffered from the withholding of the truth, for having shed tears in floods, and for having experienced the psychic pain that this causes, I reinforce my convictions about the need, to tell the truth in all circumstances, especially when it pleads on behalf of a person who has been unjustly accused.

The miracle of honesty

In my humble opinion, truth must be accessible on the same level as lies! Yes, if evil people can lie, there must be honest and good people who like to tell the truth.

LET US LOVE JUSTICE

One evening, I was attending a criminal trial with jury assistance at the Port-de-Paix Court of First Instance, where one of my cousins, bearing the same signature as me, was accused of murder. There was evidence that this member of my family had committed this heinous act. The judge who presided over the session was my teacher at the Lycée Tertulien Guilbaud in Port-de-Paix. He looked up and told me at every opportunity that he was proud of me. He looked at me in the room with great pity. I could see in his eyes all his compassion for me. He seemed to want to lighten the accused's sentence out of admiration for me.

At the moment of a short session recess, the judge received me in the private room where he was resting just before pronouncing his verdict.

"My son," he said, "I know the culprit is your cousin. I will pronounce my verdict, but you can tell me how much you'd like me to soften this sentence.

I was moved and touched by the judge's attention. But I answered him with a strong sense of justice:

"Your honor, act as if I were not in the room and properly apply what the law says; it will be justice!"

How could I want the punishment of one who took the life

of a human being to be lessened? How would I want my fame to serve as an obstacle to justice at a certain moment in time? I love justice! In my life as a sinner, I have always made many efforts not to commit injustice against anyone! All my struggles in life have always put me on the side of the weak and the needy. On the other hand, I always invite the most influential, the wealthiest, and the most powerful to show solidarity and altruism towards others.

I like this fragment of a text by the philosopher Pascal:
"It is necessary that what is strongest should be followed. Justice without force is powerless: force without justice is tyrannical. Justice without force is contradicted because there are always wicked people; force without justice is accused. It is therefore necessary to put justice and force together; and to do this, make what is just strong, or what is strong be just".

I can't count the number of times influential people with political and economic power said to me, "Daniel, you're losing a lot of privileges. Those whom you defend can be of no use to you." I have lost many privileges, but the justice that flows through me like a river gives me priceless pride and greatness. Let us love justice!

As a young entrepreneur, I am penalized by most local state actors who never award contracts to my companies for areas of service for which I have exclusivity. They penalize me because I criticize the terrible actions of the Haitian state or government. Despite this, I have never missed an opportunity to speak out against the injustice that leaders are committing, both locally and nationally. I believe that we must love justice and that there are no other options!

It is not entirely from a legal point of view that I see the term justice in this chapter; it is mainly from the point of view of fairness or impartiality in general. You have to be a lover of justice to agree to blame your friends and relatives and say that reason is on the side of the other person or your enemy.

DEFENDING JUSTICE EVEN IN FAVOR OF ONE'S ENEMIES

A few years ago, I noticed a group of young people with immense talent in poetry and street theatre. They were excellent storytellers and put on shows that didn't attract crowds since they were little known. Since I was hosting a radio show that was very popular and appreciated by the public, I asked them to come and present texts on my show every week (during the first 15 minutes) so that the public could discover them. They did. And their career was a runaway success soon after.

In 2015, I was a candidate for the Congressman position, representing the municipality of Port-de-Paix. To my amazement, these young people have been my most prominent critics during this election campaign. They were trying to denigrate me just to prevent me from getting as many votes as possible. I did not quarrel with them. They only decided to support a candidate who was more prosperous than me. Until then, it's their absolute right, and it's normal for them to

Neutrality in the face of injustice does not exist | Chapitre III

choose a candidate they feel more comfortable with. But did they need to show all this hostility against me? I don't think so! A few years after the elections, relations remained strained. There were no greetings between us. One day, I arrived at the Peace Court in Port de Paix, where I had acted as a public defender after my law studies. I attended a session at Judge Paul Blanc's locker where one of these young people was having great difficulty. This was because he did not have lawyers, and the other party's lawyer pressured him. Not knowing how to defend himself and what linguistic devices to use, he was on the verge of losing when the law was in his favor. In the meantime, all the harm he had done me was coming to my mind; I said to myself that I ought not to espouse his cause. But the moral conscience, that infallible judge lodged in each of us, began to speak to me: Daniel, you must defend justice even when it favors your enemies, for it is justice!

Under the pressure of this inner voice, I asked Judge Paul Blanc to allow me to speak and to set me up as the defender of this young man in great difficulty. When it was my turn to present evidence, I began to defend this young man's cause with such dedication that I could swing the judge's decision in his favor. The other side's lawyer and the other side were furious with me. I was increasing my enemies by defending a just cause in favor of one whom I could not consider a friend. I did so because fighting for justice is a categorical imperative. Sometimes, what is right does not appear to be the option that flatters our ego and makes us comfortable, but we must always strive to do what is right. Our conscience, which is a silent

The miracle of honesty

counselor, is faithful to its position. She gives us her opinion in any situation. It is up to us to decide whether to listen to him. When we strive to develop a certain sensitivity to justice, we feel challenged by every situation where injustice tries to establish itself. To love justice, then, is to fight injustice at all times, in all places, and against anyone!

SILENCE WHEN FACING INJUSTICE IS A GREATER INJUSTICE

Injustice has always known how to attract the silence of the majority. Many historical facts could illustrate my point. But, for the sake of argument, I retain the case of Galileo and the Catholic Church. The learned astronomer supports the Copernican thesis that the earth isn't the center of the universe but revolves on its axis and around the sun. At the time, this thesis wasn't new. It was well-known, but no one dared to support her publicly. The princes of the Church were powerful. They wouldn't accept that this theory would make them a little lost speck in the universe when they were pretending to be God's focus. Even Pope Urban VIII, who was a friend and patron of Galileo, could not prevent a trial.

The scholar is sentenced to prison house arrest, to be more precise. But also had to abjure, to renounce his hypotheses, by reading a text in which he had to acknowledge his mistakes. He was forced to contradict himself even though he was convinced of the accuracy and relevance of his reasoning. What a torment! Legend has it that after reading this, Galileo murmured, **"Eppursimuove,"** yet it turns! Men of faith who seek heaven to excess have stained the history of Christianity

Neutrality in the face of injustice does not exist | Chapitre III

with an almost indelible stain. It was not until October 31, 1992, that John Paul II, in his address to the participants in the plenary session of the Pontifical Academy of Sciences, acknowledged the errors of most theologians in the Galileo affair.

How could the entire population of the time, all the faithful of the Catholic Church, the princes, and all the authorities of such a hierarchical church, support or remain silent around such an injustice? Let us admit that Galileo's thesis was false. In what way did it endanger humanity? Were the evils inflicted on Galileo proportional to the acts he had committed? It was, from every angle, a blatant injustice.

Even today, many citizens remain silent about an injustice they witness, especially when it does not affect a close family member. To adopt such an attitude systematically rejects his humanity and human competence. It's a positioning that makes you want to vomit. Generally, when it is an authority, an essential economic actor, or someone of great renown who commits injustice, we remain silent so as not to find ourselves in front of him. Yet, these people who set the machine of injustice in motion deliberately stand in front of us and our humanity. They disrespect us. Why pretend to esteem them when they don't do the same?

To remain silent about injustice of any size is to add oil to the engine of the powerful machine of injustice, whereas it would weaken if it met with the slightest resistance. I know what I'm

The miracle of honesty

talking about. I have taken enormous risks defending ordinary citizens, anonymous people, and peasants against authorities who have the power to throw me in jail or persecute me. It's not that I wasn't aware of the risks, but I've always gotten used to the idea that I'm already a victim because someone like me is a victim!

Several people who were arbitrarily arrested and thrown in jail because a close relative, a friend, or an important person close to a government commissioner requested it have been released as a result of my fierce interventions. At times, some authorities seem to wait for an opposing voice to be raised to find a reason to release innocent people without running the risk of being perceived as traitors.

THE SLIGHTEST RESISTANCE WEAKENS INJUSTICE

A young man from Ile-de-la-Tortue, the land of my paternal ancestors, was arrested for making a speech critical of a sitting member of Parliament. Since the latter had played an important role in the process of appointing the government commissioner at the time, the young man was arrested for criminal association. Several lawyers and authorities of the judiciary saw fit to remain silent because the deputy was in office. When I learned that, after spending several days in police custody, the young man was going to be heard by the Commissioner and that he would then be brought before an examining magistrate, I quickly understood that arrangements were being made to make him spend many months in prison. Legal professionals no doubt understand the validity of my misgivings.

Neutrality in the face of injustice does not exist | Chapitre III

This investigating judge has so many cases to investigate. After how many months would he address this young man's case? I hastened to the locker of the government commissioner to make a little resistance: I know that he who commits injustice does not like to be told so; moreover, he does not have his full conviction in the act he commits.

When I arrived at the magistrate's locker, I approached him and whispered a few words in his ear. I said to him:

"Your Honor, I have come to fetch this innocent young man from your hands.

"No, Dal," he said. The situation is serious; he is accused of criminal association!

And I answered:

Tell the honorable Member that it was I who came here to demand the release of this young man. Tell him that if you don't release this young man, I will tell everyone that this arrest was dictated because of the criticism that this young man has made against him.

As soon as I had said this, the judge said to me:

"Go sit down, Dal; I must answer your quest."

I left the courthouse that day with this young man who was finally reunited with his poor, inconsolable mother, his mother unable to pay for a lawyer to defend her son. What a victory! What a triumph of justice over injustice! I can't count the number of times I've had to take a stand for people in difficult situations, abandoned by everyone, even though they were victims of injustice.

COMPLICIT THROUGH SILENCE

Failure to intervene in a situation of injustice leads us to become indirectly complicit in that injustice. Of course, by

> The miracle of honesty

positioning oneself, one runs the risk of being attacked in turn or losing certain privileges. But how can one be the friend of an unjust man if one is not, in turn, the same as him? Some people delude themselves that their silence when faced to injustice is due to neutrality. It is a great mistake to think so. One can never prove one's innocence in a situation of injustice around which one has remained silent. The immortal Martin Luther King, Jr., seems to have found the right word when he says, *"He who passively accepts evil is just as responsible as he who commits it. He who sees evil and does not protest helps to do evil."*

There can be no good reason for his silence when confronted to injustice. It does not simply disturb the individual who is its victim; it constitutes a snag on the human order. Every unjust act done, no matter where it occurs, is an attempt to destroy the entire world. The complicit silence of a single citizen, of social groups, of authorities, of a population must be understood as a kind of adherence to the destruction of humanity and the natural order. This is what **Albert Einstein**, one of the most intelligent men to have ever lived on earth, *concluded: "The world will not be destroyed by those who do evil, but by those who look on and do nothing."*

As a young, dynamic, and progressive person, growing up in a society based on an unprecedented system of social injustice, a system shaped in such a way that the harmful legacies of slave colonialism are still very much alive and powerful.

The nastiness to which I am often the victim of the Haitian customs system held hostage by powerful and corrupt

Neutrality in the face of injustice does not exist | Chapitre III

oligarchs who continually seek to establish monopoly markets, the smear campaigns to which I am sometimes subjected because I perform certain feats that differentiate me from people who make no effort, the nightmares that are often asked of me and the refusal to award public service contracts to my companies because I don't give bribes or overcharging are all symptoms of a society characterized by injustice at the highest level. The unjust punish those who do not want to play their game. Despite all that I have had to endure, despite all the evils inflicted upon me, I have never taken advantage of a single opportunity to change places with the oppressors and the corrupt. What's worse is that when I'm a victim, I can't find people to defend me, whereas every time I'm aware of an act of injustice, I rigorously denounce it. **Yehuda Bauer**, an Israeli historian, and professor emeritus, most clearly supports this position: *"You must not be a victim, you must not be an oppressor, but above all, you must not be a spectator."*

On the other hand, I find myself deeply touched by the inspired and unheard-of ideas of the Italian philosopher, Marxist intellectual, and politician, one of the highest figures of intellectual resistance in European history, **Antonio Gramsci,** who spoke out on the behavior of those who remain indifferent to the injustices, unreason, and vices of the world.

In his text **"I hate the indifferent,"** one of his first articles published anonymously in February 1917 in *La Cittafuturà*, he described indifference as cowardice and parasitism. He reveals his hatred of indifference and shows how it works

The miracle of honesty

mightily to annihilate the world with the weight of evil and injustice. He seems to have suffered powerlessly in the face of the evils and injustices imposed by the dominant social strata of the time on the underprivileged masses. The philosopher wanted to express his indignation at the indifference of his contemporaries and the rest of the world, which did not help to avoid war. If small active groups can operate, it is because the masses ignore them, but above all. After all, they do not care, he says! Gramsci skillfully used solid arguments in this text and showed little empathy for the indifferent. (See annex I) In this book, I revere the memory of this humanist intellectual who understood the role of an intellectual and the responsibilities of all citizens raised to a certain human competence. I regret, at least, that I did not have the privilege of living through the era of these men of courage and commitment. If humanity had produced only men of Gramsci's stature, that is, those who do not remain indifferent, those who think that life is synonymous with resistance, those who believe that staying silent about the lesser evil is an act of betrayal against humanity, it would be happy because men devoted to its cause would have lived. I have always imagined what the world would be like if there were no countries that exploit others and wage war against them to destroy their economies and even thousands of human lives. Let us imagine for a moment what humanity would look like if each loved and treated the other with love and compassion. Let us imagine what the world would be like if we considered the other a being to be protected as we do for our children.

Neutrality in the face of injustice does not exist | Chapitre III

I firmly believe that the face of the world can change if we work to expose injustice wherever it comes from and if we agree to stop it when we have the chance. We have the right to live in a fairer world. Let's try to invent it!

CHAPITRE IV
The Miracle of Honesty

The Miracle of Honesty

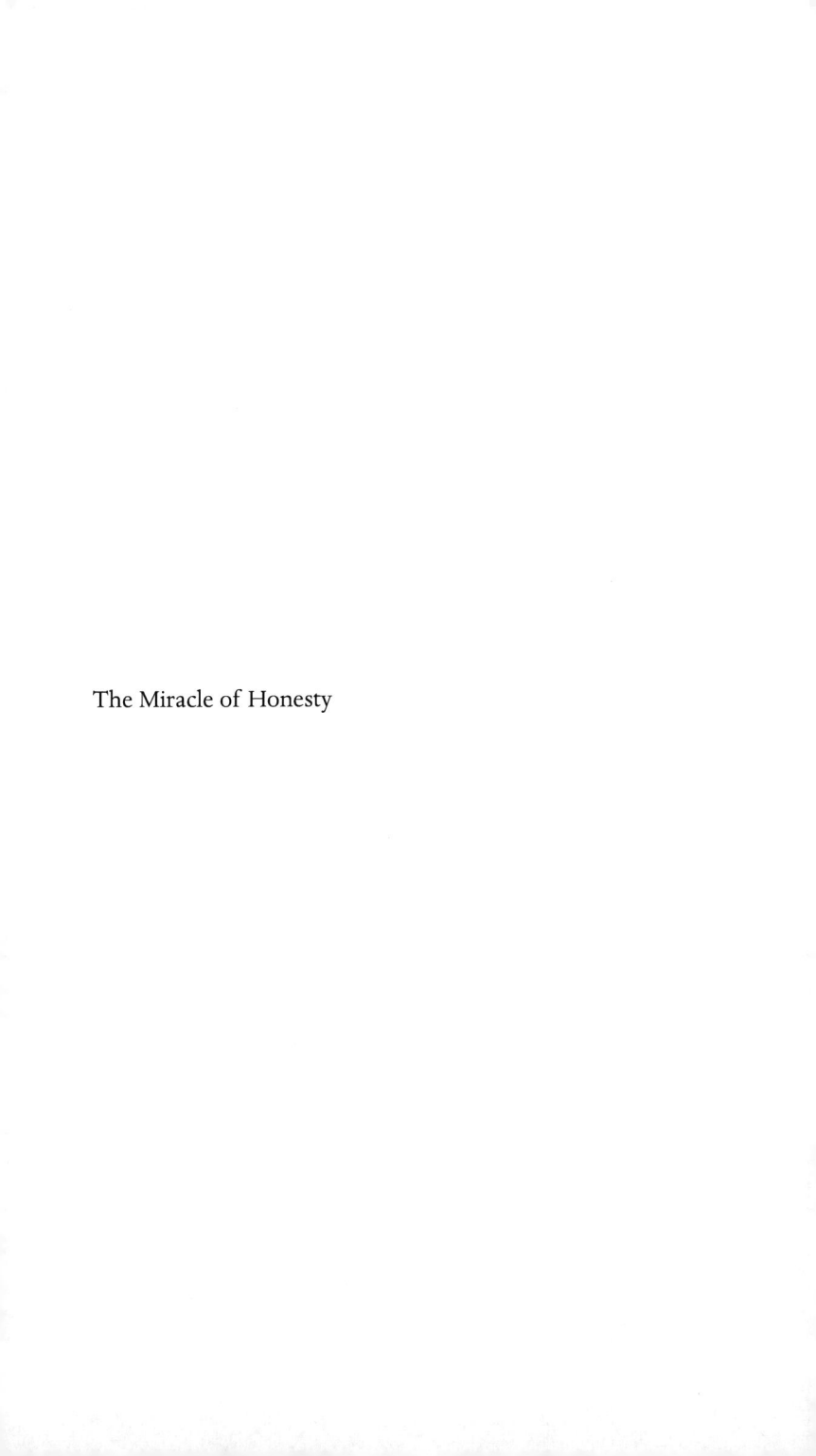

"The idea may sound laughable, but honesty is the only way to fight the plague."
Albert Camus

The miracle of honesty

A WAY OF SEEING THINGS

Honesty is generally understood as the quality of a person who acts uprightly and loyally, leads a life according to social morality and probity rules, speaks according to his thoughts, and acts in good faith. The concept can also be understood as the quality of honest behavior. This is broadly what Larousse proposes as an element of the definition. Other sources see the concept of honesty as the instinctive character that conforms with morality, virtue, and probity in one's relationship with others. The term instinctual brings a little more meaning to my understanding. Honesty, once cultivated, becomes an instinct, a reflex. It is an essential part of life skills. *"Being honest isn't just about refraining from lying, defrauding, stealing, or deceiving; it's about speaking and acting sincerely."*

The miracle of honesty | Chapitre IV

Honesty is about showing respect, integrity, and self-awareness. It is the basis of trust and social relationships. In the French seventeenth century, "honest" meant "proper, measured." The honest man, then, is the man who is decent, moderate, cultivated, and who knows how to shine in society.

In contemporary times, the meaning has not changed too much. To be honest, means to be in conformity with moral rules and established laws, to be in harmony with oneself, to be sensitive to the pleas of one's conscience, to keep one's commitments, to honor one's promises, to work for the collective welfare, to love others and to treat them justly, to recognize one's mistakes and to make amends for them, to act with love towards nature and animals, To give of oneself, to fight for justice, to espouse just causes, to love truth and wisdom.

The 3rd President of the United States of America, Thomas Jefferson, was right when he said, *"Honesty is the first chapter of the book of wisdom."* For him, honesty is the path through which to arrive at wisdom. I see at least two meanings of the word wisdom: humility and knowledge.

While consulting an online dictionary, I was excited to read a set of words synonymous with the concept of honesty: affability, amiability, friendship, propriety, benevolence, good faith, kindness, chastity, civility, conscience, propriety, decency, delicacy, dignity, distinction, gift, righteousness, accuracy, faithfulness, faith, frankness, kindness, honor, honorability, incorruptibility, integrity, irreproachability, justice, loyalty, merit, modesty, morality, morality, cleanliness, politeness, probity, modesty, purity, quality, rectitude, reserve, restraint, wisdom, scrupulousness, care, deportment, virtue. To this list, I dare add the word greatness! Honesty is a mark of greatness. It gives us hope, confidence, and compassion and improves our decision-making, actions, and words. It is that feeling which develops in us a sense of justice, balance, disinterestedness, respect for oneself and others, respect for the good of others and the public good (property of the State). It is a force of the soul and, finally, a rare skill.

IT'S NEVER TOO LATE

No matter how far along you are in the battle path to promoting and practicing honesty, you are neither behind nor too far behind. What matters most is your determination to fight this noble battle through your actions, your commitments, and the promotion of this virtue.

If, through lack of information, education, or ignorance, you have been someone who trampled on this virtue, fuels dishonest and unjust practices in one way or another, know that it is not too late to change the paradigm. To take a just or honest action is to strengthen the world and contribute to the happiness of humanity to which we all belong.

A vice of the human brain is that we never think of breaking a routine just because we have practiced it for a while. We may even believe that because our old life is known to everyone,

The miracle of honesty | Chapitre IV

it will be difficult for others to accept that we are no longer the same or that we have stopped acting as in the past. It's an effect of the brain! Get out of this vicious circle, this spiral that only aims to crush our humanity, inner consciousness, and everything that makes us extraordinarily intelligent.

Honesty shows itself. With rare ease, it provokes a marketing phenomenon known as ***"word of mouth."*** Whoever sees you acting honestly will be so amazed and touched (because it is a miracle) that he will tend to tell others about it occasionally. When you act honestly with a man or woman, he or she will be willing to defend you because he or she is speaking from experiential references. Even today, we must begin to value this virtue. The world has been in dire need of it for a long time. However, it is not too late. Let's save humanity! Let's build a brighter future for future generations and our posterity! They must not come up against the ugliness of today's world.

THE MIRACLE OF HONESTY

A miracle can be understood as an extraordinary fact or event that cannot be explained from the scientific point of view, considered supernatural, uncommon, or rare, in which one believes one can foresee an intervention of divine power. In my humble opinion, this virtue called honesty is a miracle in itself and possesses the power to work miracles. You may regard all the personal events I have given you in this book as miracles. The many feats and results that I have been able to achieve by remaining committed to honesty when doing

The miracle of honesty

otherwise would bring me the desired results more quickly and without the pain of patience are also miracles.

Let's see why I consider honesty to be a miracle in itself. Thanks to the support of digital evolution, it has become easier to defraud, lie, deceive, murder the character of those who do not like, kill, steal, and extract many advantages. As it is organized, the contemporary world facilitates the flourishing of dishonest people and advances people willing to do anything to accumulate material and financial wealth. In this system that spans the entire planet, honest people feel punished, held hostage, imprisoned, devalued, and relegated to the background. Only a supreme inner force (consciousness) and a level of excellence (taken in the sense of knowledge) are capable of aligning some people with the rank of honesty. This complex and painful choice could not fail to be a miracle, an exceptional act. If you have two cups on a table, one of which contains gall and the other honey syrup, the normal choice would be to taste the syrup. To consciously choose gall is to perform an exceptional act akin to a miracle. Paradoxically, the gall in our example represents honesty, the narrow and narrow way.

The stories told to us from the earliest antiquity, and the epoch of the infancy of humanity show a greater disposition of the majority to have recourse to maneuvers relating to vices, easiness, and all sorts of actions derived from natural liberty. Man is, by nature, selfish and prone to dishonesty. It is a miracle for one man to want to escape from his genuine will

The miracle of honesty | Chapitre IV

to dominate the other, to refuse to obtain for himself as many advantages as possible to the detriment of others and to act honestly without coercion. Even the pleasure we experience, the joy we feel, the tranquility and peace of mind that come over us after we have acted honestly testify to an exceptional state of happiness. Royal celebrations do not bring the joy that comes from a single honest act. Those who have ever savored this indescribable and dense joy know what I am talking about. Throughout the writing of this book, I have spoken with young and mature people about their state of mind after acting honestly in a given situation. Their answers are almost the same. Expressions like: *I feel good, I feel free, I feel great, I feel at peace with myself, I feel a sense of accomplishment, came up every time.*

The sense of honesty of some young people of my generation has always had a profound impact on me. I keep in mind; **Wilgens DEVILAS, Robens MAXI, Ermann SAINVIL, Bendy GENESTANT, Marie Raphaëlle PIERRE, Holdine PIERRE, Rodrigue RAYMOND, Miclaude PAUL, Ferlandanie CORNEILLE, Jefly JEAN, Suze LULLY, (Aquila) Ronald LUBIN, Louis-Dalès DESSENTIEL** and **Widson OSIAS.**

I could name dozens of names (many more), but I have chosen to mention these young people with whom I have worked and collaborated closely. In my eyes, every brutal action performed by these people to remain in on the side of honesty is a miracle in a world where virtues are in perfect decay and putrefaction. These people's lives are a powerful source of miracles for those who associate with them.

The miracle of honesty

Some have distinguished themselves before me during more than ten years of friendship or professional collaboration. They constantly desire to practice this skill, this virtue that is honesty. I take advantage of this book to tell them how much they have attracted my attention through their actions and way of being. I also want to express my admiration and gratitude to them for their participation in the battle of honesty. I want them to know that the eyes of the world are on them and that they have no right to compromise or diminish their zeal.

HONESTY, LOVE, AND EMPATHY GO HAND IN HAND

I have often met people who think they can consider themselves completely honest without feeling compassion for others. It is difficult and even impossible to be honest with oneself without being honest with others, just as it is difficult to love oneself without loving others. Otherwise, what you feel would be called self-centeredness. **Victor Hugo**, in his work *Les Contemplations,* in 1856, said: *"People sometimes complain about writers who say me. Tell us about us, they shout. Alas! When I talk to you about myself, I'm talking about yourself. How do you not feel it? Ah! You fool who thinks I'm not you!»*

Suppose you have the ability to stop worrying about yourself and your family for a moment to try to understand and share the doubts, sorrows, difficulties, feelings, and problems of others. In that case, it is because you are cultivating in yourself this excellence and goodness (empathy) complementary to honesty.

The miracle of honesty | Chapitre IV

Empathy, in my humble sense, is the tenderness of the soul. It pushes us to change places with the other person to feel their pains and dispel them if we can. Even in the situation where we don't have the means to do so, we continue to share this pain. This dimension of honesty that we are talking about (empathy) is one of the values that most of Haiti's ruling elites lack. The political sector is insensitive; the economic sector practices savage and rapacious capitalism, and the intellectual elite itself, as the last bulwark, drowns in a kind of delinquent recklessness. This total lack of empathy is the real source of all the disparities, all the scourges, all the injustices, all the instability, and all the turbulence that is eating away at Haitian society.

HONESTY AS A SOURCE OF MUTUAL AID

Last year (2022), I came across a video posted on Facebook by journalist **Wilgens DEVILAS**, where a 73-year-old widow recounted her woes, her eviction from a house because she could not pay her annual lease equivalent to 50 US dollars. I felt deeply touched. For me, this situation was a kind of reminder of the social injustice suffered by the entire Haitian population. I wondered how an old lady could live 73 years on earth without having a place to sleep. Tears streamed from my eyes, and I felt the desire to help her. According to one account in the Bible, the question of habitat was an important topic even for Jesus, the most mythical man to have passed through this earth. In Matthew 8 verse 20, he says, *"Foxes have dens, and birds of the air have nests, but the Son of Man has nowhere to lay his head.* »

The miracle of honesty

I was thinking about the desolation I could see on the face of this septuagenarian and decided to build a tiny house for her when I had barely started building my own house. I shared the project on my Facebook page and asked my fans and friends to help and support this poor lady whom I didn't know at all.

Several friends sent in their contributions. And we built this house for her over the course of 5 months. I have used tens of thousands of gourdes of funds generated by my companies to finance a good part of this initiative. The rest was funded by other friends in Haiti and the diaspora, who were affected by this story.

This feeling that invaded us, this will, this ardent desire to come to the aid of this widow, is none other than empathy. Thanks to this human sensitivity, this old lady could experience the happiness of sleeping in a house of her own and better than the one from which she had been expelled.

On the day I was holding a small ceremony to thank you and hand over the key, this lady felt unspeakable joy. She called me "Dad." The 73-year-old saw a 39-year-old as a father to him. "I should be the one calling you Mom," I said. She goes one step further: *"Accept your title because only a father can build a house for his daughter."* Every time I pass by the side of the road to Aubert, she keeps calling me "daddy." It's touching!

How many times have we missed the opportunity to be a dad, a husband, a brother, a sister, a friend, a mother to someone else? May we contribute to the collective happiness of the

The miracle of honesty | Chapitre IV

human race by learning to cultivate empathy, that nobility of the soul. Let us love one another!

While presenting a French-music program in on **Radio Balade FM**, I discovered a song by Florent Pagny called "Savoir Aimer." It seems to exemplify both what love and empathy are. (See annex II)

This song has always known how to vibrate, shake, and subjugate my whole being with each listen like a drug. Listening to this song, I can't understand why I always think of those I love or those I feel compassion for, empathy, admiration, and all the people I don't even know are in a difficult situation. Love is beautiful, love is good, love is strong. It's a language. Let us cement ourselves with love so that the world becomes a fortress of brothers and sisters of a single parental lineage. When you see another, whatever his origin, color, religion, knowledge, and beauty, see in him first another "yourself," that is, your fellow man.

Imagine for a moment how you feel when others make a generous gesture towards you, when you are the recipient of attention when you are treated with care and dignity. That's how other people feel when you do all this for them. So, make a commitment to help others feel how you like: it guarantees peace and harmony.

HONESTY AS THE VICTORY OF THE SOUL OVER THE BODY

In his brilliant philosophical reflections, Socrates gives an essential place to the soul, the immaterial or intangible

The miracle of honesty

part of being. He believes that the soul is the holder of all necessary truths. Like him, I think the body is a prison for the soul: it continually tries to distort it and deprive it of all its faculties. The soul is incapable of evil or any other vice.

It is when the body succeeds in subjugating her that she becomes a powerless witness in the face of the injustices and evasions of the world. This is why the father of philosophy believes that man must practice dying every day. To die by continually detaching one's mind from one's body through the exercise of thought, meditation, and reason.

This valuable and necessary distancing gives man the ability to come into possession of the innumerable truths, knowledge, and skills that abound in the soul. When he takes this step, he becomes wise, reasoned, and therefore able to be honest, to lead a good life, a righteous life.

Throughout this literary adventure, it gives me immense pleasure to give you an idea of my perception of life, my philosophy of intelligence, and my way of seeing the world as it is today and as it could be if the human race decides to believe its actions sincerely.

I have also told you some of my experiences and journeys without wishing to give a biographical character to this book, which is intended to share testimonies and resonate with my deep attachment to loyalty and any other competence of the human soul.

The miracle of honesty | Chapitre IV

I know that many critics will have to point out the undisguised connection I have tried to make between religion and philosophy. One will ask oneself how to be, at the same time, a great lover of philosophy and a man of faith. I would reply that philosophy and the realm have abstraction in common. The better you are at abstract things, the better you understand what is not perceptible and is hardly believable. No one can grasp reality without having an advanced idea of the ideal.

I hope this book will bring some joy and comfort to my readers who may be discouraged and have lost hope of living in a better world. Like you, I am not enthusiastic about the world as it is. But I strive every day to distinguish myself and act with as much honesty as possible. I know that you can never be honest enough and that you have to make daily efforts to improve. All of us must work so that we are able to utter this quote honestly: *"Mankind will be happy because I have lived."*

With love!!!
DALBAGAY

ANNEXE I

Annex

"I hate the indifferent. Like Friedrich Hebbel, I believe "to live means to be partisans." There can be no such thing as only men, strangers to the city. He who truly lives can only be a citizen and take sides. Indifference is aboulia, parasitism, cowardice; it is not life. That's why I hate the indifferent. Indifference is the dead weight of history. It is the leaden ball for the innovator; it is the inert matter in which the most resplendent enthusiasms are often drowned; it is the pond that surrounds the old city and defends it better than the strongest walls, better than the breasts of its warriors, because it swallows up the assailants in its silty eddies, decimates and discourages them, and sometimes makes them renounce the heroic enterprise. Indifference works mightily in history. It works passively, but it works. It is fate; it is that which cannot be relied upon; it is that which overturns the programs, that which overturns the most established plans; it is the raw material, rebellious to the intelligence it stifles. What is happening, the evil that occurs to everyone, the possibility that a heroic act (of universal value) can give rise to, is not so much due to the initiative of a few who work as to the indifference, the absenteeism of many. What is happening is not so much because a few want it to happen but because the mass of men abdicates before their will, allows it to happen, allows knots to accumulate that only the sword can cut, allows laws to be promulgated that only revolt will cause to be repealed, allows men to access the power that only a mutiny can overthrow. The fatality that seems to dominate history is nothing more than the illusory appearance of this indifference, this absenteeism. Facts ripen in the shadows; a few hands, unguarded, weave the web of collective life, and the masses ignore them because they do not care about them. The destinies of an epoch are manipulated according to narrow visions, immediate aims, ambitions, and personal passions

The miracle of honesty

of small active groups, and the masses of men are ignorant because they do not care. But the facts that have matured lead to something; But the web woven in the shadows comes to its fulfillment: and then it seems that it is fate that carries away everything on its path, it appears that history is nothing other than an enormous natural phenomenon, an eruption, an earthquake of which we would all be the victims, the one who wanted it and the one who did not like it, the one who knew and the one who didn't, who had acted and the indifferent one. And he gets angry; he wants to avoid the consequences; he wants it clear that he didn't want him and was not responsible. Some whine pitifully; others swear obscenity, but almost no one asks: what if I had done my duty too? Had I tried to assert my will and advice, would what have happened have happened? But almost no one feels guilty for his indifference, his skepticism, for not having given his hands and his activity to those groups of citizens who, precisely to avoid such an evil, were fighting and proposing to procure such a good. When facing facts, most prefer to talk about ideals that are collapsing, programs that are finally collapsing, and other jokes of the same kind. In this way, they begin to absolve themselves of all responsibility. No, of course, they don't see things clearly, and they are sometimes unable to present very nice solutions to the most pressing problems, including those that require extensive preparation and time. But for being very beautiful, these solutions remain just as fruitless, and any moral gleam does not animate this contribution to collective life; It is the product of an intellectual curiosity, not of a keen sense of historical responsibility that wants everyone to be active in life, that does not admit of any form of agnosticism or any form of indifference.

|135

| Annex

I hate the indifferent, too, because their whining of eternal innocence wears me out. I ask each of them to give an account of how he has fulfilled the duty that life has given him and gives him every day, what he has done, and especially what he has not done. And I feel that I can be inexorable, that I don't have to waste my pity, that I don't have to share my tears. I am a partisan; I live, I feel in the virile consciences of my side already beating the activity of the future city that my side is building. And in it, the social chain does not weigh on a few; in it, everything that happens is not due to chance or fate but the intelligent work of the citizens. There is no one in her to stand at the window to look at while some sacrifice themselves disappear in the sacrifice. The one who stays at the window, watching, wants to take advantage of the little good that comes from the activity of a few people and spends his disappointment by attacking the one who has sacrificed himself, the one who has disappeared because he has not succeeded in what he set for himself.

I'm alive; I'm resistant. That's why I hate those who don't resist; that's why I hate the indifferent."

ANNEXE II

Knowing How to Love

Annex

Translation of **Florent Pagny**'s song **"Savoir Aimer"**

Knowing how to smile
To an unknown woman passing by
Not keeping any trace of it
Except pleasure
Knowing how to love
Without expecting anything in return
Neither esteem nor a great love story
Not even the hope to be loved.

(chorus)
But knowing how to give
Giving without taking back
Only learning
Learning how to love
Loving without waiting
Loving to take everything
Learning how to smile
Perfunctorily
Without wanting what goes with it
And learning how to live
And leaving

Knowing how to wait
Tasting this utter happiness
That you were so desperate to find
That you receive it as if by mistake
Picturing yourself believing

The miracle of honesty

To fool the fear of the void
Fixed in yourself like wrinkles.
Tarnishing the mirrors

(chorus)
Knowing how to suffer
In silence, without a whimper
Neither defense nor armor
Suffering to death wish
And picking yourself up
As you are reborn from your own ashes
With so much overflowing love
That you can forget the past

(chorus)
Learning how to dream
Dreaming for two
Just by closing your eyes
And knowing how to give
Giving without mistake
Whole-heartedly
Learning how to stay
Desiring until the end
Staying regardless
Learning how to love
And leaving
And leaving

Annex

https://lyricstranslate.com
Translation reviewed by TransIn services. Support@transinservices.com

Made in the USA
Columbia, SC
29 March 2024